How India's Small Towns Live (or Die)

*Published by*
ACADEMIC FOUNDATION
in association with

## ABOUT THE AUTHOR

**Paromita Shastri** has been an economic journalist for twenty-five years and worked in senior editorial positions at *Business Standard* in Kolkata and at *The Economic Times*, *Outlook Magazine*, and *Mint* in New Delhi. As an independent writer-editor now, she has written for various organisations, among them IFPRI, The World Bank, Planning Commission and the MS Swaminathan Research Foundation (MSSRF). She is also a translator and child rights activist. She has written an exhaustive report "Blind Alley: Juvenile Justice in India", for HAQ: Centre for Child Rights, New Delhi, and is currently looking after their research work in child budgeting and education. She has a postgraduate degree in economics as well as journalism from Kolkata.

# How India's
# Small Towns Live (or Die)

## MAKING SENSE OF MUNICIPAL FINANCES

PAROMITA SHASTRI

ACADEMIC FOUNDATION
NEW DELHI

www.academicfoundation.com

First published in 2011
by

**ACADEMIC FOUNDATION**
4772-73 / 23  Bharat Ram Road, (23 Ansari Road),
Darya Ganj, New Delhi - 110 002 (India).
Phones : 23245001 / 02 / 03 / 04.
Fax : +91-11-23245005.
E-mail : books@academicfoundation.com
www. academicfoundation.com


in association with

PRIA (Society for Participatory Research in Asia).





Cataloging in Publication Data--DK
  Courtesy: D.K. Agencies (P) Ltd. <docinfo@dkagencies.com>

**Shastri, Paromita.**
  How India's small towns live (or die) : making sense of
municipal finances / Paromita Shastri.
     P.   cm.
  Includes bibliographical references.
  ISBN 13: 9788171888344
  ISBN 10: 8171888348


   1. Municipal finance--India.  2. Intergovernmental fiscal
relations--India.  3. Small cities--India.   I. Title.

DDC 336.01454    22


Typeset by Italics India, New Delhi.
Printed and bound in India.

# Contents

# List of Tables, Figures and Annexures

## Tables

## Figures

## Annexures

# Foreword

Half the population of the world is now living in urban areas. Nearly half a billion Indians would be living in urban areas in another two decades. India's economic growth trajectory is fueled by urban services; more than half of its current gross domestic product (GDP) is being derived from the service sector. Urban habitats are becoming the engine of modernisation, growth and cosmopolitanism of India in the 21st century.

A wide variety of pull and push factors are causing rapid urbanisation around the world, and indeed in India too. Migration from rural to urban areas has increased in search of livelihood, as much for survival as for improved standards of living. Towns and cities are the destinations of such migration. As millions pour into towns and cities in India every year, the infrastructure in urban habitats is falling woefully short. Transport, water, sanitation, housing, health care, education—the whole gamut of basic services are not available to all the citizens of such towns and cities.

India's Constitution was amended in 1992 to bring in municipalities as statutory bodies mandated for regular elections and separate functions. Section IXA of the Constitution provides for the same. The 12th Schedule of the Constitution lists 18 different functions for which municipalities are responsible. Socioeconomic development of towns and cities is the central mandate of such urban local governance institutions in India.

Nearly two decades later, the state of municipal governance in India leaves much to be desired. Effective devolution of functions, funds and functionaries has not taken place in most provinces; most municipalities lack systems of data and maps for planning and monitoring their services; and staff in municipalities lacks the competence needed for governing the modern urban habitats. The finances of municipalities are in shambles; most of them do not even have a system of book-keeping on double-entry method.

Some progress on these aspects has been made with respect to large metropolitan cities and state capitals with recent support and nudging from Jawaharlal Nehru National Urban Renewal Mission (JNNURM)—the first national programme on urban development. Reform of governance in general and municipal finances in particular faces severe challenges in such large cities as well.

The plight of small and medium towns is even worse. There are nearly 4500 such towns with elected systems of governance but they have no capabilities and resources to serve their citizens in even the most elementary manner. It is towards this central aspect of municipal finance that this book speaks. It focuses on the nature of municipal finance, its possibilities and constraints in the urban peripheries of India—its small and medium towns.

Given the globalised nature of economic development today, large metropolises are attracting investments and capabilities to govern themselves. But the vast numbers of small and medium towns remain unnoticed and ignored by investors, policymakers, development planners and social activists. Nearly half of the urban population of India is at present living in these small towns; the tier 3, 4 and 5 towns are showing higher rates of consumption of goods and services. Yet, the politics in these small towns is still largely focused on the welfare of its own citizens.

Therefore, it is imperative that small and medium towns are supported, resourced and promoted in a manner that life in such habitats is dignified and livable. Unless small and medium towns of India are governed in an efficient and accountable manner, inclusive development would not happen. Concentration of populations in large cities is directly related to absence of decent life and livelihood in small and medium towns of the country. Unless municipal financing systems—revenues and expenditures—of such small and medium towns are made transparent, sufficient and accountable, locally relevant and citizen-centric development of such urban habitats would not be possible. In fact, the reforms of urban governance in the country depend largely on reforming the system of taxation, revenue collection, expenditure targeting and efficiency in service delivery in small and medium towns. Such reforms would generate autonomy, transparency, ownership and accountability of governance in municipalities of India.

It is towards that desirable future that this volume can be a potential contribution.

— Rajesh Tandon
President
PRIA

# Introduction

Spurred on by the October 2010 Commonwealth Games, the Delhi government spared no efforts to create a 'clean and green' capital to match India's growing image as an emerging global power. Even the United Progressive Alliance government at the Centre, now in its second term, has been very active in clearing slums in an effort to decongest and beautify cities and creating world-class metros. These governments, as well as many citizens like us who live in gated colonies, perceive slums and squatter settlements as places of disease, decay and danger, festering with filth and fearsome criminals.

Why have slums proliferated in Delhi and other metros? Over 1981 to 2001, Delhi's population has gone from 6 million to 13 million and Greater Mumbai's from 10 million to 18 million, according to Census figures. This increase has more to do with declining rural livelihoods and rising migration from villages and other cities than the rate of population growth and urbanisation. I too came from Kolkata with a new job in hand. Two decades later, as I write this sitting not in a slum but in a flat bought by a bank loan, I am reminded of Bertolt Brecht, "It is true: I earn my living/But, believe me, it is only an accident./Nothing that I do entitles me to eat my fill./By chance I was spared./(If my luck leaves me I am lost.)."[1]

This unabated migration process has largely bypassed the intermediate towns—peasants from rural Bihar or UP or Odisha do not migrate to Madhubani, Mirzapur or Angul. They come straight to Delhi, Mumbai, Kolkata, Bengaluru, or at least their peripheries—Noida, Gurgaon or Kharghar. Yet, it seems, the policymakers are blind to this process of migration, urbanisation and slum creation. They also ignore the key principles laid down in the Urban Housing and Habitat Policy in 2005 and reiterated in 2007: Shelter for all, economic development, quality and safe environment. India had close to 9 per cent growth for much of this decade

---

1. Brecht (1939).

and a consumer goods revolution, yet these principles have been apparently too tough to implement.

Instead, the administrators concentrate on evictions and slum clearance as part of a continuing "reforms" process that seeks to privatise all possible public space. According to a study by the Bangkok-based Asian Coalition for Housing Rights, a regional network of grassroots community organisations, NGOs and professionals actively involved with urban poor development processes in Asian cities, in 24 incidents between January 2004 and June 2005, some 854,250 people were evicted in India, mostly by governments.[2] There were several reasons for this: environmental improvement, hawker encroachment clean-up, development of land as park or redevelopment as malls and tourism development. The traumatic eviction of nearly 1.5 lakh men, women and children from the Yamuna Pushta colony in Delhi in April 2004 to a remote settlement with neither shelter nor livelihood opportunities or school is still fresh in public memory.

A major factor that has driven rapid urbanisation of big cities in India is the decline, in the eighties and nineties, of small 'mofussil' towns as centres of economic, intellectual and social activity. Only 5 per cent of China's population lives in its biggest cities, compared to close to half of India's. While China has invested heavily in providing small clusters of urban amenities and economic infrastructure, India has chosen to look on silently while its small towns and cities stagnate and villagers flock to the metros in search of better opportunities. They prefer to sell their little pieces of land and work as delivery boys, security guards, even construction labour in the metros, eking out a squalid existence in slums.

In the Visundarpur slum in Mirzapur, UP, 350 households living a stone's throw from the well-appointed bungalows of government officers, have no electricity, water or sanitation. Their houses are semi-permanent and the men work as daily wage labour.[3] Why then would they not shift to Delhi?

There are many ways in which India can be urbanised systematically and even the small towns revived. We can begin by improving the civic and

---

2.   *http://www.achr.net/Evictions%20Asia/Trends%20Evictions%202005.html*

3.   Sharma (2009).

municipal amenities in the district/block headquarters. A parallel step would be to create 'urban' clusters that attract human capital and investment and encourage people to shift from subsistence farming to other professions. This can be done by creating an environment that sustains not only the basic minimum conditions of living such as water, electricity, housing, etc., but fosters those extra social and economic incentives that drive people's aspiration and dynamism of existence, such as education, entertainment, retail, services and so on.

When China began to reform its economy in 1978, it had an urbanisation rate of barely 18 per cent (roughly equivalent to India in 1950). Thirty years later, the proportion is estimated around 55 per cent! In India, urbanisation has been slow to begin with, mainly for reasons mentioned above and lack of land development for urban housing. But there are now signs that this may be changing. According to the Ministry of Urban Development, more than half of the people in India are going to live in cities and towns in the next two decades. Development will cause urbanisation whether we like it or not.

Mike Davis has written in his *Planet of Slums* that the present trends indicate a creation of underclass of workers who are excluded from the formal economy constituting a permanent class of the dispossessed.[4] About one billion of the world's population lives in slums but according to UN-HABITAT projections, this figure is likely to double by the year 2030. This means that one-third of humanity could be living without security of tenure, and health or sanitation facilities in the near future, many of them in India.

It is to prevent this urban dehumanisation that policymakers need to look at reviving India's small towns and urbanising the big villages. For that, the health of the municipalities and the process of their constitution and their working must change. They also need power to work with some independence, with effective devolution of functions, funds and functionaries happening from the state level. At present, most small town municipalities are in shambles; they lack resources, planning, data, maps, incentives and proper accounting. Corruption and power politics dog them, while the citizens, for whom they exist, have no say or role in their

---

4. Davis (2007).

functioning. The ambitious urban reform programme called JNNURM too bypasses them.

This book is a sincere attempt to look at the whole gamut of municipal finances in India, keeping the small towns as its core. It documents the slow—even lack of—change, in the devolution of power to the bottom tier of the governance systems, especially in urban areas. It argues that effective citizen participation is mandatory to bring about the force of change in India's towns and cities. Participatory Research in Asia (PRIA), a civil society organisation that has been working towards strengthening urban governance in small towns in 12 states of India and demystifying, reading and assessing municipal budgets since 2000, is the spark behind this book. A detailed study by PRIA that managed to unearth data with great difficulty from practically informally operating municipal bodies in 30 small towns forms the centre of this discourse.

I am grateful to Dr. Rajesh Tandon, President, and Dr. Kaustuv K. Bandopadhyay, Director, PRIA, for giving me this opportunity to turn this study into a book and for fuelling my desire to delve deeper into the unfinished devolution of governance in India, which has always bemused and baffled me. Writing this book, essentially a labour of love, has strengthened my belief that power flows not out of the barrel of a gun, not even out of ballot papers, but from the mind of enlightened and empowered citizens who actively seek a stake in governance. I dedicate this book to them.

— Paromita Shastri<br>
New Delhi

# Will India Miss the Global Bus?

## *Urbanisation and its Demands on Local Bodies*

Rapid economic liberalisation in India and a substantial rise in average per capita income since the nineties, which have principally benefited the urban areas, have contributed to an intense population pressure on Indian cities and towns. As people have moved continuously from rural areas in search of a better life and economic opportunities, fueled by declining productivity and income from an agriculture that has turned sensitive to global commodity prices, urban infrastructure has crumbled in protest. This in turn has led to various bottlenecks in—and often denial of—people's access to public services as well as failing municipal governance in big cities as well as small and medium towns. At its current stage of economic development, the lack of an overt and visible urban prosperity and efficient administration is keeping India from competing with other emerging powers such as China, to become a preferred destination for both foreign capital and tourists. More importantly, it is keeping the country from optimally utilising its urban productivity potential. Concentration of population and economic activity is considered crucial for leveraging certain external economies that in turn facilitate improvement in productive efficiency, technological innovations and access to global markets.[1]

Aware of this, the Central government launched the prestigious JNNURM in 2005, to promote rapid and systemic reform of urban infrastructure and administration through strengthening of municipal governments and their functioning in accordance with the provisions of the 74th Constitution Amendment Act, 1992, during the Eleventh Plan period

---

1. Kundu (2006).

(2007-2012). India's winning bid to host the Commonwealth Games in 2010 has added fire to this drive, especially in the capital city of Delhi where every attempt is being made to bring infrastructure and governance up to global metropolitan city standards. Indirectly, this has also put the spotlight on smaller urban centres where inadequacies of resources and governance are far starker than in Delhi—in fact, even practically absent in a few of them.

## The Rise and Rise of Urban Areas in Developing Countries

Even as expanding economic opportunities have helped cap population growth in the industrialised West, urban areas in developing countries are going through a population explosion. According to a joint study by UN-HABITAT and Economic Development Institute of the World Bank,[2] despite significant steps to reduce rural-urban migration, the rate and scale of urbanisation continues to be massive and unprecedented. In just the last quarter of the twentieth century, the population of these urban centres in developing countries has grown by one billion. While individual cities in India are growing by 250,000 to 500,000 people every year, its total urban population is estimated to go up by an astounding 100 million in the next 12 years. In other words, seven cities of the proportion of Mumbai must be created to accommodate this increase. As per Census 2001, India has 35 cities with a population of a million plus each, and although they are home to only 38.6 per cent of the total population (see Annexure Table A-1.1), together they generate about 60 per cent of the income.

According to the Ministry of Urban Development, the urban population of India is expected to reach a staggering 575 million by 2030, from 325 million in 2005 as estimated by the UN population database. Sanjeev Sanyal, founder, Sustainable Planet Institute, WWF, says, "Within 2025, states such as Tamil Nadu, Maharashtra, and possibly Punjab and Gujarat will have an urban majority, while within 2040-2045, the entire country will have an overall urban majority."[3] Urbanisation on such massive scale involves setting aside larger and larger shares of the total

---

2.  UN-HABITAT and World Bank (1990).

3.  *http://www.business-standard.com/india/news/sanjeev-sanyal-building-cities-for-21st-century-india/365959/*

public spending for servicing dense human settlements, even if for no reason other than accomodating rising vote shares and health concerns. Rising population also demands more water, electricity, sanitation, road space, telephones, transport and other public services. As the costs of providing these are high, the growth of large cities often involves diseconomies of scale in some kinds of infrastructure. Long pumping distances for water in water-scarce Delhi as well as commuting distances for work area in the case of geographically narrow Mumbai are good examples of such diseconomies. This has led indirectly to promotion of very costly and private water supplies and a bankruptcy of the government-owned water distribution authority in Delhi, while in Mumbai, land and property costs have shot through the roof even in remote places as more and more residences come up to accommodate the huge throngs of commuters.

As a result, "urban areas in developing countries are demanding rates of investment that are far higher than those achieved (or needed) by the cities of Europe and North America during their periods of rapid growth".[4] This investment need is slated to go up due to the changing concepts of urban planning, especially the growing need for environmentally sustainable towns and cities with low per capita ecological footprint. The combined demand for heavy investments along with high current expenditure places heavy strains upon the absolute levels of public resources, adds to political conflicts over the allocation of resources between regions/towns, and forces a realignment of national investment priorities towards programmes to raise prosperity and reduce poverty in villages to reduce pressure on urban areas. In India, the expensive seven-point Bharat Nirman rural infrastructure programme was launched in 2005 for precisely this reason.

There are two financial consequences of the above. The first is the need for cities—and urban local bodies—to generate as much as possible of the resources needed for investment and current spending. And the second is the need for public agencies to make the most effective use of resources (and investment) wherever possible and avoid waste or leakage. Also, in order that such attempts to generate public revenue in cities do not add to

---

4.   Ibid.

the burden of the poor, public expenditure must give priority to the types of service provision that benefits the poor.

**Table 1.1**

*Trends in Urbanisation in India, 1951-2001*

| Census Year | Total Population (Millions) | Urban Population (Millions) | Share of Urban Population in Total Population (Per cent) | Decadal Urban Growth Rate (Per cent) | Compound Annual Growth Rate | | No. of Urban Agglomerations/ Towns |
|---|---|---|---|---|---|---|---|
| | | | | | Total | Urban | |
| 1951 | 361.08 | 62.44 | 17.29 | - | - | - | 2822 |
| 1961 | 439.23 | 78.93 | 17.97 | 26.41 | 1.98 | 2.37 | 2334 |
| 1971 | 548.15 | 109.11 | 19.91 | 38.24 | 2.24 | 3.29 | 2567 |
| 1981 | 683.32 | 159.46 | 23.34 | 46.15 | 2.23 | 3.87 | 3347 |
| 1991 | 846.30 | 217.61 | 25.71 | 36.47 | 2.16 | 3.16 | 3769 |
| 2001 | 1027.02 | 285.35 | 27.78 | 31.13 | 2.11 | 3.11 | 4378 |

*Source:*  National Institute of Urban Affairs (2000). *Urban Statistics: Handbook 2000.* New Delhi, January and Census 2001.

Studies show that most urban areas in the country have seen deterioration in the standard and quality of public life. In almost every urban centre, irrespective of size or class, the availability of basic services has declined, and a huge number of people in specific settlements such as slums or resettlement colonies have no access to most of the services and amenities.

**Table 1.2**

*Urban Agglomerations/Towns by Class/Category*

| Class | Population Size | Number of UAs/Towns |
|---|---|---|
| Class I | 1,00,000 and above | 393 |
| Class II | 50,000-99,999 | 401 |
| Class III | 20,000-49,999 | 1,151 |
| Class IV | 10,000-19,999 | 1,344 |
| Class V | 5,000-9,999 | 888 |
| Class VI | Less than 5,000 | 191 |
| Unclassified | | 10* |
| All classes | | 4378 |

*Note:*  * Data is provisional.

*Source:*  Ministry of Urban Development and Census 2001. *http://urbanindia.nic.in/DMU/main.htm*

**Table 1.3**

*Growth of Various Classes of Towns in Respect of Growth
of Urban Population*

| | No. of Towns | | | | | Percentage of Urban Population to Total Population | | | | |
|---|---|---|---|---|---|---|---|---|---|---|
| *Class of Town* | *1961* | *1971* | *1981* | *1991* | *2001* | *1961* | *1971* | *1981* | *1991* | *2001* |
| > 100,000 | 113 | 148 | 216 | 300 | 393 | 9.22 | 11.38 | 14.04 | 16.5 | 15.50 |
| 50,000 to 99,999 | 138 | 183 | 270 | 345 | 401 | 1.97 | 2.20 | 3.00 | 2.80 | 3.34 |
| 20,000 to 49,999 | 484 | 582 | 739 | 947 | 1151 | 2.99 | 3.23 | 3.11 | 3.62 | 4.43 |
| 10,000 to 19,999 | 748 | 874 | 1048 | 1167 | 1344 | 2.26 | 2.10 | 2.24 | 2.02 | 3.37 |
| 5,000 to 9,999 | 761 | 678 | 742 | 740 | 888 | 1.20 | 0.90 | 0.80 | 0.69 | 1.12 |
| Below 5,000 | 218 | 178 | 230 | 197 | 191 | 0.14 | 0.09 | 0.11 | 0.07 | 0.04 |
| Unclassified | | | | | 10 | | | | | |
| All classes | 2462 | 2643 | 3245 | 3696 | 4378* | 17.78 | 19.67 | 23.30 | 25.70 | 27.80 |

*Note:* * Includes 10 unclassified towns.

*Source:* Office of the Registrar General, India.

It is imperative to have urban infrastructure for improved productivity
in the urban area. In India, the local governments are primarily responsible
for such infrastructure provisions. However, the local government's
capacity and capability in mobilising resources, delivering services more
effectively and equitably and in promoting local economic growth is
inadequate. The focus on financing the urban infrastructure has been more
on the service side interventions in the form of various financing
arrangements with relatively less emphasis on strengthening the local
governments.

The task before municipalities in most developing countries is to raise
adequate revenue for both capital investment and recurrent expenditure,
employment of staff, operation and maintenance of facilities and servicing
of debt. However, raising revenues fairly is also important, as inequity
increases resistance from the people who feel they are being asked to pay
more in taxes or charges or do more than they can afford or in proportion
to the type and quality of the services received.

However, till today, municipal bodies in general are not seen to be
showing an active interest in expanding their resources. Many of them
continue to be sick and taxes remain their principal source of income.

Innovativeness, restructuring and efficiency are the goals that still remain a distant dream.

## Types of Urban Local Bodies (ULBs)

Despite tremendous variations in character, almost all towns and cities in the world have a representative or quasi-representative system of local government. The variations are in two important areas:

a) *The relationship of municipal boundaries to urban settlements.* In some cities such as Mumbai or Nairobi, a single local authority has been responsible for the core city and virtually all suburban development. Some others such as Kolkata and Manila, by contrast, represent cities fragmented between a few municipal jurisdictions.

b) *The extent of municipal functions.* Refuse collection, market administration, local road maintenance, cleaning, drainage, lighting, parks and recreation are virtually always municipal responsibilities. What varies widely is municipal involvement in:

   i) Public utilities, chiefly water and sewerage (provided sometimes by a national corporation, or typically by a metropolitan corporation or, a municipally controlled enterprise) and electricity distribution (usually a national public or private utility company is responsible but can be a function of local government);

   ii) Social services (municipalities often provide primary schools and health clinics but their role diminishes beyond that in the case of secondary schools and hospitals);

   iii) Public protection (fire services are frequently municipal, but police forces are often state responsibility);

   iv) Highways and trunk roads, which can be a national or state responsibility;

   v) Provision of housing (can be a municipal activity or of a special purpose authority);

   vi) Regulation of land use and development (usually municipal but can be metropolitan or state authority function).

## Evolution of Municipal Bodies/ULBs in India

The responsibilities and functions of the city-state in India—what they are and should be—were first talked about in Chanakya's well-known treatise in statecraft, *Arthashastra*, which was written in the third century BC. However, our present urban local government bodies owe its genesis to the British rulers. India's first known municipal corporation dates back to 1688. It came up in the city of Madras, now called Chennai, by dint of a Royal Charter. It was followed, much later, by the municipal corporations in Calcutta and Bombay in 1726. But the municipal bodies that we see in our cities now owe their form and structure to a resolution adopted on 18 May 1882 by Lord Ripon, then governor general of British India, in which municipal authorities for the first time were given responsibility as units of self-government.

After Independence, the Constitution of India was framed on federal principles. Those who drafted the Constitution divided the gamut of government functions into three long lists, demarcating responsibility to Federal, State and Concurrent lists. Local government bodies are covered by the State List and thus fall exclusively under state government domain. These are governed by the state statutes—or in the case of the Union Territories by the Union Parliament.

Unlike the functional jurisdiction of the states, which follow a Constitutional delimitation, the functional domain of local bodies is derived from the responsibilities delegated by the State, which are not mandatory. Until the Constitutional amendments in 1992 and respective state legislature amendments in 1994, municipal authorities were organised on the basis of the *ultra vires*[5] principle. The state governments were free to extend or control the functional sphere through executive decisions, without an amendment to the legislative provisions. Local self-government issues continued as an exclusive subject of the state governments and the Centre never intervened.

---

5. In administrative law, an act may be judicially reviewable *ultra vires* in a narrow or broad sense. Narrow *ultra vires* applies if an administrator did not have the substantive power to make a decision or it was wrought with procedural defects. Broad *ultra vires* applies if there is an abuse of power or a failure to exercise an administrative discretion (e.g., acting at the behest of another or unlawfully applying a government policy).

Till 1992, local governments acted as agencies of state governments. In rural areas, Panchayati Raj Institutions (PRIs) informally provided basic community and judicial services while in urban areas, municipal authorities served the purpose. The political and economic environment during the late 1980s and early 1990s forced the local authorities to depend fiscally and financially on the state as well as the Centre to finance their overall development activities in the form of guarantor to their loans. This very likely forced the hand of the Centre, leading to its direct intervention in local self-government issues and ultimately encouraged it to introduce the 73rd and 74th Constitutional Amendment Acts (Part IX-A of the Constitution of India) that gave sweeping powers to the local authority, especially in planning and development by involving people at all levels. While the 73rd Amendment, also known as Panchayati Raj Act, empowered the village assemblies called *panchayats*,[6] the 74th, Amendment, popularly known as the Nagarpalika Act, sought to strengthen the ULBs.

The Constitution defines a municipality as an institution of self-government constituted under Article 243Q. A municipal area means the territorial area of a municipality as is notified by the governor of the state. Article 243Q of the 74th CAA requires that municipal areas shall be declared having regard to the: a) population of the area, b) the density of population in that area, c) the revenue generated per annum for local administration, d) the percentage of employment in non-agricultural activities, and e) the economic importance of the local body or other such factors as may be specified by the state government by public notification for this purpose. This Article further divides ULBs into three major categories: municipal corporations for larger areas, municipal councils, including municipality, municipal board, municipal committee for smaller areas and *nagar panchayats*, including town area committees and notified area committees, for transitional (rural to urban) areas. No quantitative dimension for area or population has been specified for their identification.

---

6.   *Panchayat* literally means an assembly of five people to look after a village or a cluster of villages. Panchayati Raj is a three-tier governance system, in which *gram* (village) *panchayats* are the basic units of administration, going up to block and district levels. The number of members usually ranges from 7 to 31. This is an elected body with 33-50 per cent reservation for women and for minority communities. The head of a *panchayat* is called a *pradhan/sarpanch*. The block-level institution is called the *panchayat samiti*. The district-level institution is called the *zilla parishad*.

By 1994, all states amended their own Acts to meet with the emerging political, legal and administrative issues. ULBs are now governed by the Municipality and Corporation Acts of the respective states. Several states have specified their own criteria for the purpose—their legislatures setting up the criteria while amending their Acts. For example, Karnataka has laid down that all the *taluka* (block) headquarters be given the status of *nagar panchayats* irrespective of their population, whereas Uttar Pradesh has adopted norms that define urban areas on the basis of density of population, revenues earned by the local bodies and the share of non-agriculture. Workforce can be notified as the government may deem fit.

## Empowering ULBs

Along with globalisation and liberalisation, decentralisation has also become a major plank of public policy all over the world in recent years. Devolution is an important component of decentralisation. It means the transfer of authority for decision-making, finance and management to autonomous units of local government. It involves transferring responsibilities for services to local bodies that elect their own representatives, raise their own revenues, and have independent authority to make investment decisions.

The 73rd and 74th Amendments to the Constitution gave the ULBs an elective status as well as power to impose taxes—mainly property taxes in urban areas. Education, housing and land use, development of industrial and commercial estates, and electricity distribution are some of the functions that have been decentralised in urban areas.

In fiscal terms, the municipal sector in India is a tiny fraction of the Indian economy (the 1992 Amendment does not apply to Meghalaya, Mizoram and Nagaland as they already have traditional forms of local self-government). According to the Twelfth Finance Commission report, there are 3,723 ULBs, of which 109 are municipal corporations, 1,432 are municipalities and 2,182 *nagar panchayats*. The total revenue of these ULBs grew from Rs. 11,515 crore[7] in 1998-99 to Rs. 15,149 crore in 2001-2002 at a compound average growth rate (CAGR) of 9.6 per cent. Their

---

7. A lakh is a hundred thousand, a crore is ten million and 100 crores make a billion.

total expenditure increased from Rs. 12,035 crore to Rs. 15,914 crore during the same period, registering a CAGR of 9.8 per cent.

International comparisons of local government revenues are hazardous, but a look at municipal revenues in some other countries only highlights the sorry state of affairs in India. According to a Reserve Bank of India study in 2008[8] on municipal finances in India, aggregate revenue of all ULBs in India, is very low at around 0.75 per cent of the country's GDP. In contrast, the ratio is 4.5 per cent for Poland, 5 per cent for Brazil and 6 per cent for South Africa (see also Table A-1.5 in Annexure I).

According to the seminal and brilliant work[9] by O.P. Mathur and Sandeep Thakur on India's municipal sector, the sector accounted for only 0.63 per cent of the gross domestic product (GDP) in 2001-02. More importantly, in 2001-02, municipalities generated approximately Rs. 12,750 crore, or 3.07 per cent of the total publicly-raised resources in India. This gives an idea of the enormity of the task at hand in terms of reforming the sector.

## Composition of ULBs

The municipal corporations and municipalities are fully representative bodies, which means the members must be elected popularly, while the *nagar panchayats* can be either fully or partially nominated bodies. The 74th CAA stipulates that the seats in all the constituencies in municipalities shall be filled in by persons chosen through direct election. Alongside, it also provides for representation of Members of Parliament (MPs), Members of the Legislative Assembly (MLAs) and persons having special knowledge of municipal administration, according to the discretion of the state legislature.

For example, in Chhattisgarh the composition of the municipality is followed by the formation of the council/committee. The committee consists of:

- A president,
- A vice-president,

---

8.   Mohanty *et al.* (2008).

9.   Mathur and Thakur (2004).

- Councillors,
- A chief municipal commissioner.

Apart from them, the state also nominates the following:

- One Lok Sabha member from the state,
- One Rajya Sabha member from the state,
- Two aldermen.

Unlike the functional jurisdiction of the states, which follows a Constitutional delimitation, the functional domain of local bodies, including municipal governments, is derived from the responsibilities that are delegated by the states through the legislature. This is done on the basis of Article 243W of the Constitution read with the Twelfth Schedule, as detailed in Box 1.1. Besides the 18 items listed as municipal responsibilities in the Twelfth Schedule, the legislature of a state, by law, can assign any tasks relating to: a) the preparation of plans for economic development and social justice, and b) the implementation of schemes as may be entrusted to them. The provisions of this article are not mandatory and it is for the legislature of a state to decide as to which powers and authority it may devolve on a municipality.

The legal-institutional framework for the delivery of civic services in cities and towns as envisaged in the 74th Amendment also comprises a number of mandatory institutions:

- State Election Commission (Article 243K);
- Municipalities: municipal corporations, municipal councils and *nagar panchayats* (Article 243Q);
- Ward committees and other committees (Article 243R);
- State Finance Commission (Article 243I);
- District Planning Committee (Article 243ZD) to make development plans for the district; and
- Metropolitan Planning Committee (Article 243ZE) to make development plans for metros.

However, the responsibility for creating and commissioning this legal-institutional framework, including the institutions above and parastatals impacting on civic service delivery has been left to the state governments.

## Box 1.1

*Powers, Authority and Responsibilities of Municipalities (Article 243W)*

Subject to the provision of this Constitution, the Legislature of a State may, by law, endow

(a) The municipalities with such powers and authority as may be necessary to enable them to function as institutions of self-government and such law may contain provisions for the devolution of powers and responsibilities upon municipalities, subject to such conditions as maybe specified therein, with respect to:

   (i) The preparation of plans for economic development and social justice;

   (ii) The performance of functions and the implementation of schemes as may be entrusted to them including those in relation to the matters listed in the Twelfth Schedule.

(b) The committees with such powers and authority as may be necessary to enable them to carry out the responsibilities conferred upon them including those in relation to the matters listed in the Twelfth Schedule.

**Twelfth Schedule functions:**

1. Urban planning, including town planning;
2. Regulation of land use and construction of buildings;
3. Planning for economic and social development;
4. Roads and bridges;
5. Water supply for domestic, industrial and commercial purposes;
6. Public health, sanitation, conservancy and solid waste management;
7. Fire services;
8. Urban forestry, protection of the environment and promotion of ecological aspects;
9. Safeguarding the interests of weaker sections, including the handicapped and mentally retarded;
10. Slum improvement and upgrade;
11. Urban poverty alleviation;
12. Provision of urban amenities and facilities, such as parks, gardens, playgrounds;
13. Promotion of cultural, educational and aesthetic aspects;
14. Burials and burial grounds, cremations, cremation grounds and electric crematoriums;
15. Cattle pounds, prevention of cruelty to animals;
16. Vital statistics, including registration of births and deaths;
17. Public amenities, street lighting, parking lots, bus stops and public conveniences;
18. Regulation of slaughterhouses and tanneries.

*Source:* National Institute of Urban Affairs (NIUA) (2005).

The 73rd and 74th Constitutional Amendments have given some potency to the movement towards decentralisation below state level all the way down to the *gram panchayats* and ward committees. While this is a major step towards local accountability, as yet effective decentralisation is largely absent in most parts of India although a few states such as Kerala and West Bengal have made further progress in this regard. Interestingly, while moving the Constitution Amendments in Parliament, former Prime Minister Rajiv Gandhi had envisaged that the role of the bureaucracy at the grassroots level would have to be 'liquidated' to enable the institutions of self-government to take roots.

Very few administrative functions and even fewer sources of independent finances have been devolved to the local governments, and state level bureaucrats and politicians still largely hold sway.[10] That in states such as Kerala and Bengal this decentralisation has been somewhat more effective than in other states has much to do with the fact that prior land reforms and political awareness movements in these two states have made capture of local governments by the oligarchic local elites slightly more difficult. Economist Pranab Bardhan[11] says, "While fiscally responsible and locally accountable governments at panchayat level remain one of the major ways of deepening India's democracy, much will depend on how far we can proceed in our campaign for land reforms to weaken the powers of the local oligarchy, expansion of education, a more vigorous devolution of finances to local governments and regular auditing and activation of local non-government organisations."

## The Objective of the Book

The canvas of the 74th CAA is much larger than what this book is trying to restrict itself to. Important aspects of the Amendment relate to local electoral processes, composition of local bodies, establishment of district planning committees and ward committees, municipal and state finances, and devolution. The book concerns itself only with the state of municipal finances in India, the reasons behind this poor state (including devolution and state transfer issues), and an analysis of the constraints in

---

10.   Bardhan (2007).

11.   Ibid.

the ways of improvement. The analysis, however, is oriented towards small and medium towns, where India's future urban expansion will take place and where the darkness is more under the lamp than around it. In this, we take the help of a large sample study of small and medium towns in several states conducted by PRIA, a civil society organisation which is working for over 25 years in the field of people and community participation to improve governance.

It is clear that there is an urgent need to improve the finances of municipal bodies if India has to address its urban infrastructure problems and increase the potential for optimum utilisation of urban productivity. Yet, much of this is not possible without local bodies having direct power or at least proper devolution of financial powers. Only a few countries have a discrete list of functions and fiscal powers for municipalities. Brazil and Nigeria are among such countries where municipalities draw powers directly from the Constitution. Even in India, besides acquiring a Constitutional status, legitimacy and protection, the municipal system has not undergone any structural change after the 74th CAA. Worse, as Mathur and Thakur point out, there are little signs of any redistribution or realignment of powers between municipalities and state governments. "Without questioning the merits of decentralisation and simultaneously affirming that local government reform is an integral part of the decentralisation strategy, large segments of the government administration appear to believe that maintaining the status quo or even reinforcing the mechanisms of control over the local government system is preferable to stronger local governments."[12]

Several civil society organisations, notably PRIA and its partners, have been working in the area of more participatory local self-government. For the past eight years, PRIA has worked in strengthening urban governance in 12 states of India and in demystifying, reading and assessing municipal budgets. Several studies, mainly exploratory in nature, were conducted to raise the knowledge base on the status of municipal finances in these states. These were followed up by a bigger study to further streamline and deepen the knowledge about municipal finances in small and medium towns as well as to understand the dynamics involved in citizen

---

12.   Mathur and Thakur *op. cit.*

participation in the fiscal processes. The outcome expected was to help bring about improved functioning of municipalities as well as enhance citizen participation.

Within the broad framework of financial reforms to be carried out at the Centre and state level, this particular study advocated financial and other supporting reforms of urban local bodies so as to lead to effective governance, urban prosperity and higher growth. The long-term goal was to generate greater transparency and accountability of the local bodies, bringing about greater efficiency in revenue generation as well as improved provision of basic services, and performing the range of functions devolved and entrusted to them through the respective state acts.

The specific objectives of this study were:

- Enhancing knowledge of existing revenue sources and expenditure patterns of ULBs, and

- Exploring opportunities and potentials to enhance revenue sources and suggesting better fiscal management for ULBs, including exploring the extent to which citizens can participate in urban governance.

The methodology involved a detailed survey of literature and study of the Municipal Act and relevant public documents to examine the municipal finance scenario at the state level. For the case studies, the following steps were involved:

- Collection of municipal finance data (mostly from municipal budget documents, and sometimes from financial records kept by the municipal officers or the state government directorates of urban development) for five most recent years of the ULB—the analysis has been carried out by both functional and financial heads.

- Interviews of municipal functionaries and other citizens on financial priorities of the ULB, their opinion on level of service provision and the extent of people's participation in the budgeting process.

- The analytical reports were made at three levels—detailed city-level reports for the towns covered as case studies, as well as consolidated reports at the state level and an integrated national report.

Since these municipalities' ability to provide quality basic services to its citizens as well as to perform the range of functions devolved through the respective state Acts will depend on efficient fiscal governance and management, PRIA's conscious strategy was to work with selected small and medium-sized municipalities in each of these states with the ultimate goal of making them transparent and democratic in functioning and accountable to the citizens as well encourage the citizens to get involved and actively participate. Earlier research had revealed that without legal provisions and real spaces for citizen engagement in the fiscal areas of local governance, the effectiveness and impact of citizen participation are restricted. In fact, even where legal frameworks are in place, if citizens do not take advantage of these processes to engage in governance, outcomes may be disappointing due to the underlying inequalities and power differentials. A better informed citizen can

- Engage better with local governments to secure material advantage for poorer groups and consolidate democratic practice at local levels, and

- Make elected representatives from these governance institutions more responsive and accountable to people's needs.

However, the study discovered that it was still too early to explore the possibility and scope of active citizen's participation in any meaningful manner, mainly because the municipalities had yet to travel a great distance to achieve efficient fiscal management that would make them self-sufficient enough to operate with a fair degree of independence and plan for the long term. Citizens too were found to be apathetic. They did not have any direct participation, representation being through the elected representatives, who too are most of the time not sensitive to citizens' needs.

The study was carried out in eight states, namely Rajasthan, Odisha, Andhra Pradesh, Haryana, Himachal Pradesh, Madhya Pradesh, Chhattisgarh and Bihar. (The study was also carried out in Gujarat but the results were not included in the final report because of data problems. Lack of data did not allow financial analysis for Bihar and extensive interviews were taken of a wide variety of stakeholders of urban governance.)

In each state except Haryana, Andhra Pradesh and Odisha, five small or medium towns were chosen for case studies. Two urban local bodies, one *nagar panchayat* and one municipal council, were taken up for detailed study and analysis.

**Table 1.4**

*List of Towns Included in the Study*

| Name of the State | Sl. No. | Name of the Town | Population (2001 Census) |
|---|---|---|---|
| Bihar | 1 | Sasaram | 131172 |
| | 2 | Raxaul | 41610 |
| | 3 | Madhubani | 3575281 |
| | 4 | Kanti | 20871 |
| | 5 | Motipur | 21957 |
| Chhattisgarh | 1 | Kharsia | 17388 |
| | 2 | Kawardha | 32495 |
| | 3 | Dantewada | 6641 |
| | 4 | Janjgir | 32513 |
| | 5 | Dongargaon (not included due to poor financial data) | |
| Haryana | 1 | Karnal | 221236 |
| | 2 | Sonepat | 225074 |
| | 3 | Narnaul | 62077 |
| | 4 | Mahendergarh | 24323 |
| Himachal Pradesh | 1 | Parwanoo | 8609 |
| | 2 | Nagrota Bagwan | 5657 |
| | 3 | Bilaspur | 13058 |
| | 4 | Dharamshala | 19124 |
| | 5 | Manali | 6265 |
| Madhya Pradesh | 1 | Sehore | 92518 |
| | 2 | Mandsaur | 117555 |
| Rajasthan | 1 | Aklera | 18172 |
| | 2 | Bhilwara | 280128 |
| | 3 | Bilada | 38661 |
| | 4 | Karauli | 66239 |
| | 5 | Jhunjhunu | 100485 |
| Andhra Pradesh | 1 | Mahbubnagar | 130849 |
| | 2 | Anakapalle | 84523 |
| Odisha | 1 | Angul | 38018 |

## A Brief Background to Small and Medium Towns of India

Owing to inadequate capacity and capability of mobilising resources, India's state governments have usually found it difficult to deliver urban services effectively and equitably. Traditionally, financing arrangements by state governments have been attempted more to provide external funding arrangements through service side interventions to local governments than strengthening the latter's own abilities and making them accountable for their budget balances. For instance, realistic user charges for basic services provided have been neglected for so long that many urban bodies are neither able to deliver such services properly nor raise charges for services so badly delivered.

As a result, municipal finances in India generally are in shambles, and worse in the case of urban local bodies in small and medium towns. Except for Maharashtra and Gujarat, there is no state where municipalities are able to raise revenues that cover their own expenditures. The expenditure-revenue gap is particularly high in such states as Madhya Pradesh, Rajasthan, Uttar Pradesh and West Bengal.

In the backdrop of the existing state of municipal finance, one can predict that the future trajectory of development of a town will be, to a great extent, determined by its economic base and potential. A little over three-fifths of 285 million urban Indians, said Census 2001, or 177 million stay in about 2000 small and medium towns. Unable to compete with the agrarian stories of India's vast rural areas, small and medium towns have suffered unfairly in the hands of researchers, administrators and policymakers alike. Even the media shifts its lenses towards them only when something sensational happens, although the Mumbai film industry has finally woken up to the potential, both cinematic and pecuniary, of stories located in these towns, as exemplified by the wide and critical success of films such as *Bunty Aur Babli, Jab We Met, Manorama Six Feet Under* and *Oye Lucky Lucky Oye*, to name a few.

The 2001 census lays down specific criteria that determined the urbanity of any settlement. These are: a) it should have a population of at least 5,000, b) the population density should be greater than 400 persons per square km, and c) over 75 per cent of the male workers ought to be in non-agricultural occupations. The upshot of this is many towns in India are smaller than villages, stuck in a transitory phase with a curious mix of traditional occupations, modern technology and changing social mores and attitudes. Mobile phone stores and beauty parlours coexist with cattle sheds and handpumps for water and latest models of automobiles honk through extremely narrow, maze like streets. This is partly a result of declining urbanisation in India over the eighties and nineties; urbanisation rate declined from 3.8 per cent in the seventies to 3.1 per cent in the eighties and 2.7 per cent in the nineties.[13] From all indications, it has picked up in the latter half of this decade, but statistics to back this are still not available.

Except those in fast-growing Haryana, all states in the study have lower urbanisation than the national average. Himachal Pradesh is mountainous and Bihar towns face economic and urban stagnation. Chhattisgarh is rapidly urbanising while Rajasthan has seen bigger towns growing at the expense of small and medium ones. However, all the towns, in their own way, have adequate potential to be the focal points of economic prosperity for the surrounding region. But to achieve that, a standard level of basic services has to be provided, which they are mostly unable to provide because of the fiscal mess.

Many of the towns surveyed have evolved from marketplaces for agricultural produce of surrounding regions, such as Kharsia in Chhattisgarh and Sasaram in Bihar. Some grew around small industries. For instance, Mirzapur in Uttar Pradesh is a renowned centre for classical handicrafts made of brass, utensils and carpets and also works as a *mandi* or market town for the neighbouring villages. Parwanoo in Himachal Pradesh developed around processed food industries and Bhilwara in Rajasthan has been the centre for textile mills for long, while Motipur in Bihar grew because of a sugar mill. Even now in Sehore, where a private sugar mill and paper mill were shut down because of lack of water, workers awaiting payment of dues carry on a relay hunger strike in front of the court. Globalisation, allowing corporate entry into retail marketing, has impacted places like Sehore that were once important *mandi* towns. Just outside Sehore, ITC has set up its e-Choupal that caters to all needs of rural communities from tractors and fertiliser to groceries, luring people away before they can enter Sehore.

Some towns like Dantewada and Kawardha in Chhattisgarh have developed as informal settlements providing services to pilgrimage centres. Towns in Haryana have benefited from their proximity to Delhi, while some developed by dint of their own status, as did Dharamshala as the administrative headquarters of Kangra district of Himachal Pradesh. Yet,

---

13.  Kundu (2006).

many of these now lie in a state of utter disrepair and helpless neglect, even as slums skirt their boundaries and threaten to envelop them.

Except in Bihar and Himachal Pradesh, where there is wide diversity among the towns chosen, the towns surveyed display an inherent natural strength which is waiting to be developed into their USP by an efficient municipal management. In Rajasthan, they have a wide base for small industries and sport archaeological (Bhilwada) or pilgrimage sites (Jhunjhunu) that can become focal points for tourism. Towns in Madhya Pradesh have similarly very rich potential for tourism development but suffer from water scarcity (Sehore). Chhattisgarh towns too hold great promise for tourism for its natural splendour of forests, topography, waterfalls and are the focal points of tribal folk culture and offering a prolific scatter of important pilgrimage centres, religious festivals and shrines. The hinterlands of almost all towns have great wealth of mineral resources.

By contrast, the towns surveyed in Haryana have witnessed recent rapid land development and have thriving markets, mostly for their respective agricultural hinterlands. Some towns in Himachal Pradesh have good bases for industry, trade and tourism. Some towns in Bihar display tremendous potential for economic prosperity given their natural resources, or their strategic location. None of the towns surveyed, however, have reached their potential for development. A primary step towards that goal would essentially involve consolidation of urban governance to ensure smooth and efficient provision of basic civic services.

A large part of the scarce resources of the urban local bodies are also frittered away by an omnipresent corruption which throttles urban governance and city development. However, its magnitude, nature and character vary widely from state to state. Also, nowhere is there any evidence of direct citizens' participation, particularly in planning and budget making processes. On the one hand, councillors are neither approachable nor sensitive to the needs of the citizens, and on the other, even most of the citizens have utter apathy towards governance.

Yet, most of these towns hold immense potential for developing as vibrant urban centres with perhaps a judicious mix of proper resource allocation and optimal use of resources, good planning, an informed governance and an aware and participating citizenry. Small towns are still not as polluted, crowded, stressful and impersonal as India's biggest cities, which pamper the rich and are indifferent to the less fortunate. A beginning in sustainable economic livelihood options and good governance can launch a virtuous cycle to attract people and business. The efforts made by PRIA and its partners in over 60 small towns in 12 states point to this. These organisations have helped establish, through a process of citizen consultation, *mohalla samitis* (area committees) and tried to fill the absence of data by conducting surveys and assembling information on resources and services available. PRIA has helped these towns to put in an efficient management system in place for basic services such as registration of births and deaths and solid waste disposal, helped prepare town maps and district development plans, built capacities of elected local representatives and used the municipal finance studies to educate and inform representatives, many of them first time in office, about budget formulation and management.

## Municipal Finances: Neglect by Design and Default

Chapter 8 of the Twelfth Finance Commission report highlights how, despite several attempts, there is no source of reliable data on finances of all local bodies in India to estimate their resource gaps, forcing the TFC to fix the total amount of grants-in-aid to local bodies on an ad hoc basis. Availability of firm and comparable data on municipal bodies in India is poor and do not facilitate proper assessment of their finances. There have been a few comprehensive studies of municipal revenues and expenditure in India. Four studies need particular mention. The 2003 study by Mukesh Mathur of NIUA on strengthening municipal finances outlines several reform pathways but is dated now. A broad idea of the current state of municipal finance is available in the Twelfth Central Finance Commission (TFC) report, 2005. Also, O.P. Mathur and Sandeep Thakur's excellent study that was commissioned by the TFC (mentioned above), brings out a very high level of dependence of all types of urban local governments and actually advocates a change in the constitution. The study carried out by P.K. Mohanty and others (also mentioned above) under the tutelage of the Reserve Bank of India and published in January 2008 is extremely comprehensive and the latest on this topic.

All these studies have brought out the helpless dependence of ULBs on transfers and grants-in-aid from state governments and expressed concern at the negligible share of local own source revenues (tax and non-tax) in the expenditures. For instance, in 1991-92, revenue raised by the municipalities formed 4.6 per cent of the revenue raised by the Central government and 8.05 per cent of the revenues raised by the state governments. In 2001-02, the size of the municipal sector measured in terms of revenues that the municipalities generate by way of levy of taxes, duties, fees and fines was estimated at Rs. 1,27,48 crore. These revenues formed 3.07 per cent of the publicly-raised resources, the shares of the Central government and all state governments combined being 57.5 per cent and 39.5 per cent respectively. As a proportion of the combined GSDP, own revenues of municipalities came to only 0.63 per cent.

Among the states, it varied between the highest levels of 2.16 per cent of GSDP in Maharashtra and 0.07 per cent of GSDP in Bihar. Over the five-year period, the size of the municipal sector has registered a marginal expansion, both in terms of its share in total publicly-raised revenues and in combined GSDP. Municipal share in the total revenues of the three tiers of government has risen from 2.84 per cent in 1997-98 to 3.07 per cent in 2001-02, while its share in GSDP has increased from 0.61 per cent to 0.63 per cent during the same period. Municipal own revenues (nominal terms) have risen at an annual average growth rate of 10.32 per cent.

The same pattern is visible in the aggregated expenditure levels of municipalities. As a proportion of the GSDP, municipal expenditures have risen slowly from 0.74 per cent in 1997-98 to 0.75 per cent, 0.77 per cent and 0.75 per cent respectively in the successive years. On an average, municipal under-spending in relation to Zakaria Committee[14] norm is 130 per cent,[15] which probably explains the extremely low level and quality of services offered. "Independent of the norms too, average per capita expenditures (daily) ranging between Rs. 0.20 and Rs. 2.25 cannot, by any standard, be expected to deliver services that would satisfy the needs of either

---

14.  Municipal expenditure norms were developed in 1963 by the committee of ministers constituted by the Central Council of Local Self Government headed by Rafiq Zakaria, which have been widely used to assess municipal under-spending. However, these norms are now outdated by technological changes in municipal services.

15.  Mathur and Thakur *op. cit.*

the urban households or other non-domestic consumers. With the exception of Maharashtra and Gujarat, there is no state where municipalities are able to raise revenues that are adequate for meeting local expenditures."[16]

Thus, reforms have to be initiated so that in the long term, the municipal bodies emerge financially self-sufficient. For this, tax reforms should be initiated to improve tax collection, particularly property tax collection. User charges and fees should be charged on the basis of more realistic and cost effective rate, so that non-tax incomes are consolidated. And technological and accounting changes should be made compulsory to prevent corruption, promote transparency and better governance and facilitate further reforms.

In the next two chapters we discuss the current status of funds, functions and functionaries at ULBs in India, the Constitutional fiscal devolution process, the inherent constraints in the federal system of funds flow, the limits imposed upon the state and the local governments and the efforts made—or the lack thereof—by the Central and state finance commissions to fill the gaps in the funds flow process, raise flow of resources to local governments and strengthen their financial position. Two subsequent chapters discuss in detail the revenue and expenditure situation of ULBs in general and those of the towns in the study in particular. The sixth chapter analyses the reform efforts undertaken so far by ULBs and other reform options in the entire municipal finance system, with clear recommendations for future. The concluding chapter tries to outline a way ahead for urban local governments to function well and efficiently, while strengthening resource mobilisation and distribution, and explores the possibility of using effective citizen participation to reach that goal.

---

16. Mathur and Thakur *op. cit.*

# 2   A Constitutional Dependence

*Local Bodies in Search of Space
in India's Fiscal Federalism*

Fiscal decentralisation is defined as the devolution of taxing and spending powers to lower levels of government. Specifically, it refers to the principles and practices concerning functional or expenditure responsibilities, revenue assignment and rectification of vertical and horizontal imbalances.[1] Broadly, then, fiscal decentralisation is the fiscal empowerment of lower tiers of the government, the municipal bodies and the PRIs at the grassroots.

In a federal structure of government, national/central governments assign more expenditure functions to the sub-national/state/provincial governments than the sources of revenues.[2] The same is true of the latter which assigns more responsibilities to their local governments than their revenues require. The result is the mismatch between functions and finances, called a 'vertical imbalance' in theory. This makes downward transfers inevitable to meet the fiscal gap. Still, it is widely accepted that transfers should not be "gap-filling" as far as possible nor should it bail out the incompetent and the irresponsible, but should take into account the criteria of needs, rights and incentives. Fiscal autonomy cannot be built in a regime of grants.

Notwithstanding the theoretical requirements of decentralisation and devolution, local governments in India continue to wallow in a fiscal grey area. The 74th Constitutional Amendment demarcated the functional domain of municipal authorities but neglected to provide for a corresponding 'municipal finance list' in the Constitution. The failure to

---

1. Mohanty *et al.* (2008).

2. Bird *et al.* (1995) observed quoting international experience that stable systems of inter-governmental relations are characterised by clearly stated expenditure assignment rules, rather than by the subjective decisions and murky assignments that define the inter-governmental systems in many countries.

do this has forever skewed the finance situation of urban local bodies. According to the RBI study,[3] "The assignment of finances has been completely left to the discretion of the State Governments, excepting in that such assignment shall be 'by law'. This has resulted in patterns of municipal finances varying widely across States and in a gross mismatch between the functions assigned to the ULBs and the resources made available to them to discharge the mandated functions." Thus, for everything from assignment of revenue sources to provision of transfers and allocation for borrowing with or without state guarantees, the ULBs have to depend on the state government. This dependence in turn extends from the state governments to the Union government, as Figure 2.1 shows.

**Figure 2.1**

*Fiscal Dependence of Urban Local Bodies*

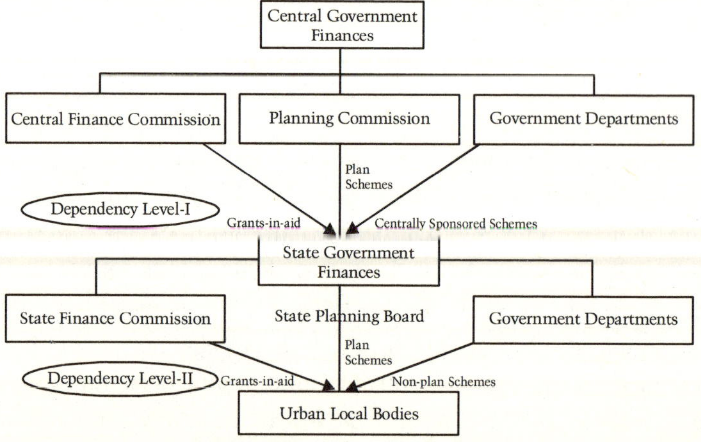


*Source:* Reserve Bank of India, Study no. 26.

Much like the asymmetry between the Centre and states, there is a marked asymmetry between states' and local governments' revenue raising powers. If decentralisation has taken place, it is more at the level of expenditure than revenue generation (see Figure 2.2 for sources of ULB finance) and the financial status of urban local bodies remains as pitiable as ever. Says economist Amrita Dhillon,[4] "A disproportionate share of

---

3.  Bird *et al.* (1995).

4.  Dhillon (2007).

expenditure at local levels is incurred by urban local bodies compared to rural areas where mostly grants from central ministries are spent."

**Figure 2.2**

*Financing of Municipalities*

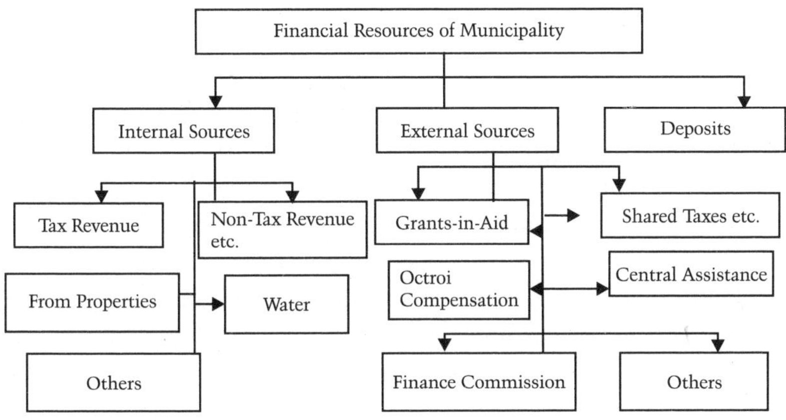


## Sources of Funds for ULBs

The provision of the financial structure of the municipality shows that it depends both on the internal and the external sources for funds. The internal sources depend upon tax revenue and non-tax revenue from its own sources while the external sources have grants-in-aid and the shared taxes and other forms of financing to the municipalities.

### Taxes

There could be four types of local taxation:

- Taxes that municipalities impose by their own legislation;

- Taxes levied under national legislation but with tariffs determined by municipalities (either freely or within statutory limits);

- Taxes that municipalities assess and/or collect;

- Taxes levied and administered by Central government but whose proceeds are given to, shared with or surcharged by municipalities.

### Government Transfers

A lot of resources with municipal authorities are allocations of funds from national governments to local ones or development authorities responsible for urban services and development. There are also transfers from state or provincial governments to local authorities. Such inter-governmental transfers take many forms.

- *Capitalisation:* The investment of equity capital by Central government in a local authority which is expected to utilise it for income-earning projects, such as utilities, markets and slaughterhouses. Such equity may be transferred or sold to others but it is not repayable by the recipient. It may, however, be expected to yield dividends for the Central government as investor. Urban development authorities and utility corporations are frequently financed in this manner, and Central government may also invest equity in undertakings administered by provincial or local governments.

- *Tax-sharing:* The allocation of specific Central government revenues to local government. Some of these are made under revenue-sharing obligations laid down in federal constitutions. Nigeria, for example, distributes 15 per cent of federal revenues to local governments. Even the Philippines, not a federation, allocates 20 per cent of net national internal revenue to local government.

- *Grants, subsidies, contributions or subventions:* All names for transfer of funds from the budget and accounts of the Central government to those of a self-accounting local authority. These are usually discretionary payments as while such grants may be a part of the Constitution, the amount of the payment is not usually prescribed by law.

## Functions of ULBs

The municipal bodies are vested with a long list of functions delegated to them by the state governments under the municipal legislation. These functions broadly relate to public health, welfare, regulatory functions, public safety, public works and development activities. Public health includes water supply, sewerage and sanitation, eradication of communicable diseases, etc.; welfare includes public facilities such as education, recreation, etc.; regulatory functions related to prescribing and enforcing building bylaws, encroachments on public land, registration of births and deaths, etc.; public safety includes fire protection, street lighting, etc.; public works measures such as construction and maintenance of inner city roads, etc., and development functions related to town planning and development of commercial markets.

In addition to the legally assigned functions, various departments of the state government offer to assign unilaterally, and on an agency basis, various functions such as family planning, nutrition and slum improvement, disease and epidemic control, etc. The Twelfth Schedule of the Constitution (Article 243W) provides an illustrative list of 18 functions that includes the traditional core functions of municipalities as well as development functions, such as, planning for economic development and social justice, urban poverty alleviation programmes and promotion of cultural, educational and aesthetic features. However, conformity legislations enacted by the state governments indicate wide variations in this regard.[5]

## Little Uniformity, Much Confusion

The transfer of funds along with the functionaries is the key to achieving the goal of functional decentralisation. Without adequate fund and strong functionaries, the ULBs cannot possibly discharge their responsibilities effectively. Yet, some 17 years after the two CAAs, there exists a wide variation in functions and responsibilities provided in the Statutes of states. The current status of transfer of functions in ULBs in four states is detailed in Table 2.1.

There is no uniformity, and activities are confused with subject and departments. Also, transfers of functions and responsibilities vary widely across the states and among the different tiers of local bodies. Part of the confusion arises because some of the subjects are drawn from the concurrent list where there is commonality of interests of Central, state and municipal governments, as Table 2.2 shows, and the 1992 CAA does little to sort out this confusion.

---

5.   NIUA (1998a).

**Table 2.1**

*Functional Devolution for Urban Local Bodies in Four States*

| Functions Prescribed in the 12th Schedule | Status of Functions and Departments that Execute Them | | | |
|---|---|---|---|---|
| | Haryana | Himachal Pradesh | Rajasthan | Chhattisgarh |
| Urban planning including town planning (marginally devolved) | TCPD | TCPD | TCPD | TCPD |
| Regulation of land use and construction of buildings | PWD | TCPD | ULB | PWD |
| Planning for economic and social development, construction of buildings | ULB | TCPD | ULB | ULB |
| Roads and bridges | ULB, PWD | PWD | ULB | PWD |
| Water supply for domestic, industrial and commercial purposes | PHD | IPHD | PHED | PHED |
| Public health, sanitation conservancy and solid waste management | ULB | ULBs | ULB & health dept. | PHED & malaria dept. |
| Fire services | ULB | Fire dept. | ULB | ULB |
| Urban forestry, environment protection and promotion of ecological aspects | ULB | Forest dept. | ULB | ULB |
| Safeguarding the weaker sections, handicapped, mentally retarded | ULB, Social welfare dept. | Public welfare dept. | ULB, Social welfare & WCD | ULB, State welfare dept. |
| Slum improvement and upgrade | ULB, SUDA DUDA | ULB | ULB, Tourism dept. | ULB |
| Urban poverty alleviation | ULB | ULB | ULB | ULB |
| Provision of urban amenities and facilities—parks, gardens, playgrounds | ULB | ULBs | ULB planning, ownership, construction & maintenance | ULB planning, ownership, construction & maintenance |
| Promotion of cultural, educational and aesthetic aspects | ULB, Dept. of school education | Public relations Dept. | ULB | ULB |
| Burials and burial grounds, cremations, cremation ground and electric crematoriums | ULB | ULB | ULB | ULB |
| Cattle pounds and preventions of cruelty to animals | ULB planning, ownership, construction & maintenance | ULB | ULB planning, ownership, construction & maintenance | ULB planning, ownership, construction & maintenance |
| Vital statistics including registration of births and deaths | ULB | ULB | ULB | ULB |
| Public amenities—street lights, parking lots, bus stops and public conveniences | ULB | ULB, SEB & HRTC | ULB | ULB |
| Regulation of slaughterhouses, tanneries | ULB | ULB | ULB | Not devolved |

*Note:* TCPD - Town and Country Planning Department; PWD - Public Works Department; PHD - Public Health Department; IPHD - Irrigation and Public Health Department; PHED - Public Heath Engineering Department; WCD - Women and Child Development; SUDA - State Urban Development Authority; DUDA - District Urban Development Authority; SEB - State Electricity Board; HRTC - Himachal Road Transport Corporation.

*Source:* "Democratic Decentralisation of Urban Governance", *PRIA Occasional Paper* series No.4, 2009.

**Table 2.2**

*Schedule 12 Functions in the Concurrent List*

| Function | Entry |
|---|---|
| Planning for economic and social development | 20 |
| Urban forestry, protection of the environment and promotion of ecological aspects | 17(A and B) |
| Safeguarding the interests of the weaker sections of the society, including the handicapped and mentally retarded | 16 |
| Cattle pounds and prevention of cruelty to animals | 17 |
| Vital statistics including registration of births and deaths | 30 |

Municipalities depend upon their own funds and the help from the state governments from time to time. Own funds are certain and called recurring income, while help from the state government is uncertain and called non-recurring income. Recurring income covers all the taxes, tolls and other ways of income collected by the municipalities. Non-recurring income includes grants, compensations (octroi, etc.), loans, grants from the Central government, all finance commissions, etc.

In most of the smaller municipalities in India, the recurring deposit is low, hampering development work and other schemes. As the non-recurring income is not timely, the municipal authorities' main concern relates to meeting pay, allowances and other expenses. But even in the socially progressive state of Kerala, where the literacy rate is high, tax collection is low and the municipal bodies depend upon the grant and compensation from the state. Out of all the municipalities studied, the PRIA study found that only one municipality had a sound deposit base of its own.

## Role of CFCs and SFCs in Devolution of Funds and Functions

Effective decentralisation can be achieved only through devolution of resources and the functional responsibilities to the third tier of governance or the grassroots level, so that at the lowest level decision-making powers offer socioeconomic benefits and help in mobilising more resources and efficient delivery of access and services. The in-built fiscal imbalances between the Central government and state governments in India and in

**Figure 2.3**

*Funds Flow to Urban Sector in a State*

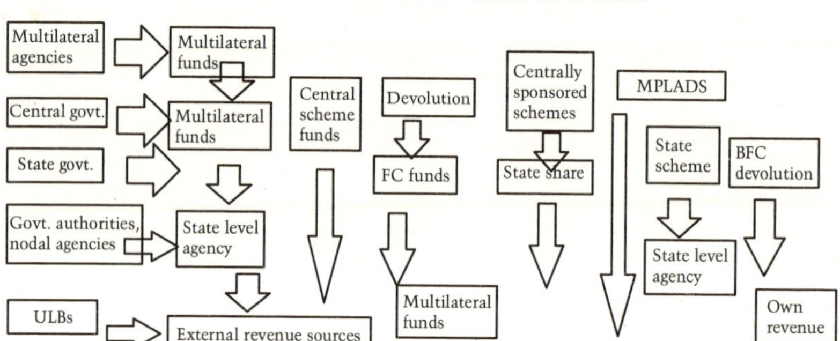


turn, between state governments and local governments, are usually
bridged through the mechanism of transfer of resources from higher levels
to lower. This mechanism is devised, and built as well as improved upon
every five years, by a Constitutional body called Central Finance
Commission at the Central level and the state finance commissions at the
state level. So far, 12 CFCs have given their reports and the Thirteenth
Finance Commission (2010-2015), headed by economist and former senior
bureaucrat Vijay L. Kelkar, submitted its report in February end, 2010.[6]

## How CFCs Helped Change States' Fiscal Health

For the first time, it was the Eleventh Finance Commission (EFC)
(2000-2005) which was mandated to suggest measures to augment the
consolidated fund of the states to enable them to supplement the resources
of the local bodies. But even the Tenth Finance Commission (1995-2000)
had made recommendations in this regard, beyond its terms of reference
(ToR), as Article 280 had been amended during its term. It was of the view
that measures to augment the consolidated funds of the states for
*panchayats* and municipalities need not necessarily involve transfer of
resources from the Centre to the states. Still, it recommended a grant of
Rs. 100 per capita of rural population as per the 1971 census for the
*panchayats* and Rs. 1,000 crore for the municipalities on the basis of the
inter-state ratio of slum population derived from the 1971 census.

---

6.   The recommendations came too late to be incorporated in this book.

## Table 2.3

*Criteria and Weights used by EFC and TFC for Inter Se
Distribution of Funds*

| S.N. | Criteria | Weight (Per cent) | |
|---|---|---|---|
| | | EFC | TFC |
| 1 | Population | 40 | 40 |
| 2 | Geographical areas | 10 | 10 |
| 3 | Distance from highest per capita income | 20 | 20 |
| 4a | Index of decentralisation | 20 | - |
| 4b | Index of deprivation | - | 10 |
| 5 | Revenue effort | 10 | 20 |
| | (a) with respect to states' own revenue | 5 | 10 |
| | (b) with respect to GSDP | 5 | 10 |

*Source:* EFC and TFC reports.

The EFC recommended a number of measures, such as assignment of land tax, profession tax and surcharge or cess on state taxes for improving basic civic services and implementing schemes for social and economic development. Reforms were recommended in respect of property tax/house tax, octroi/entry tax and user charges. While it did not see the need for making any additional provision for this, it also recommended ad hoc annual grant of Rs. 1,600 crore for *panchayats* and Rs. 400 crore for municipalities, to be spent ideally on activities such as maintenance of accounts, development of database and audit and any remainder on core civic services.

Of late, central finance commissions have been concerned more with ensuring macroeconomic stability than simply working out resource transfer formulas. The EFC was told to review public finances and suggest ways to restructure them to restore budgetary balance and maintain macroeconomic stability. It was also asked to design a "monitorable programme of reducing deficits" after it submitted the report. The TFC was asked to recommend a fiscal restructuring plan to help the Union and state governments phase out their revenue deficits and reduce fiscal deficits to a manageable level. The new Thirteenth Finance Commission has been asked to "...suggest measures for maintaining a stable and sustainable fiscal environment consistent with equitable growth". In fact, then finance minister P. Chidambaram, in his 2008-09 Budget speech, went so far as to request the Commission "...to revisit the roadmap for fiscal adjustment and suggest a suitably revised roadmap". This is a worrying trend and has been triggered perhaps by the success of the EFC formula in getting states to balance their books, though mostly by fiscal persuasion.

Based on the recommendations of the EFC, the Government of India had instituted a fiscal reform facility (FRF) for the states for the period of 2000-01 to 2004-05. Many states took refuge behind this and set their financial houses in order, often by neglecting necessary social sector expenditure. The improved fiscal health of both the Centre and the states in the current decade reflects the effect of this engineering, though since 2008-09 the central fiscal deficit is wayward again. The estimated aggregate gross fiscal deficit relative to GDP has declined from 8.4 per cent in 2003-2004 to 5.5 per cent in 2007-08, while the revenue deficit is down from 5.9 per cent to 1.3 per cent. This was also achieved through a huge increase in income tax and service tax revenues at the central level, which in turn led to higher tax devolution and grants from the Centre to the states.

The increased transfers from the Centre combined with two positive developments in most states. One, the introduction of the value added tax buoyed revenues in several states. Second, states' interest payment liability came down on account of debt-swap and write-off schemes introduced as part of the FRF. These factors exerted a downward pressure on the aggregate fiscal deficit of the states, which slumped to 2.3 per cent in 2007-08, from 4.4 per cent in 2003-04. And the revenue deficit became a thing of the past; from 2.3 per cent of GDP in 2003-04, the states together reached a marginal surplus in 2007-08. This was a sea change from the near-bankruptcy situation that prevailed in the states in the late nineties and signals a significant turnaround in state finances, despite the heavy off-budget liabilities existing at both Central and state levels which, according to some economists, could constitute an additional five per cent of GDP.[7] The deficits in some states such as West Bengal still remain high, while some states, as mentioned above, have brought down their deficits by compressing developmental expenditures. This has, ironically, happened more in states with poor tax income which leaves little leeway in managing resources.

---

7.   Rao *et al.* (2008).

The 80th Constitutional Amendment replaced the devolution of selective central taxes by general tax sharing, leading to discontinuation of separate assignment of additional excise duties. The TFC has therefore recommended the distribution of 30.5 per cent of net proceeds of central taxes. The entire 30.5 per cent is to be distributed according to a uniform formula given in Table 2.4.

### Table 2.4

*Criteria and Relative Weights for Tax Devolution:*
*Twelfth Finance Commission[8]*

| Criterion | Weight (Per cent) |
|---|---|
| 1. Population | 25 |
| 2. Income (distance method)* | 50 |
| 3. Area | 10 |
| 4. Tax effort** | 7.5 |
| 5. Fiscal discipline*** | 7.5 |

*Note:* *The distance method is given by: $(Y_h\text{-}Y_i)P_i / \Sigma_i (Y_h\text{-}Y_i)P_i$ where, $Y_i$ and $Y_h$ represent per capita SDP of the $i^{th}$ and the highest income state respectively and $P_i$ is the population of the $i^{th}$ state.

** Tax effort $(\eta)$ is estimated as $(\eta) = (T_i / Y_i) / (0.5\ 1/Y_i)$ where, $T_i$ is the per capita tax revenue collected by the $i^{th}$ state and $Y_i$ is the per capita state domestic product of the $i^{th}$ state.

*** estimated as the improvement in the ratio of own revenue of a state to its revenue expenditures divided by a similar ratio for all states averaged for the period 1966-1999 over 1991-1993.

Interestingly, Rao *et al.* argue, finance commission transfers, even if on gap-filling basis, have been so far more equitable than the Planning Commission system. In fact, discretionary transfers have increased of late with the Planning Commission and various central ministries making grants for both general and specific purposes under Article 282 of the Constitution. The normal assistance to state plans given under the Gadgil formula[9] declined from 85 per cent of state plan assistance in 1991-92 to 27.5 per cent in the budget of 2008-09. This is definitely a cause for worry, more so because own revenues of the states are adequate to finance only 56

---

8. Rao *et al.* (2008).

9. The Gadgil formula distributes funds keeping in view four objectives: (i) population control and maternal and child health; (ii) universalisation of primary education and adult education; (iii) on-time completion of externally aided projects; and (iv) success in land reforms. For a detailed explanation, see *http://pbplanning.gov.in/pdf/gadgil.pdf*

per cent of their current expenditures. All the rest of it is financed by transfers, which have been going down as is clear from Table 2.5.

### Table 2.5

*Composition of Central Transfers to States (in Percentage Share)*

| Plan Periods/ Years | Finance Commission Transfers | | | Plan Grants | | | Other Grants | Total |
|---|---|---|---|---|---|---|---|---|
| | Tax Devolution | Grants | Total | State Plan Scheme | Central Scheme | Total | | |
| Fourth Plan (1969-1974) | 54.4 | 10.3 | 64.6 | 12.9 | 11.6 | 24.4 | 11.1 | 100.0 |
| Fifth Plan (1974-1979) | 50.2 | 17.1 | 67.3 | 17.7 | 11.7 | 29.4 | 3.3 | 100.0 |
| Sixth Plan (1980-1985) | 57.0 | 5.1 | 62.1 | 17.7 | 16.6 | 34.3 | 3.6 | 100.0 |
| Seventh Plan (1985-1990) | 54.2 | 6.9 | 61.0 | 17.0 | 18.1 | 35.1 | 3.9 | 100.0 |
| Annual Plan (1990-1991) | 52.2 | 10.5 | 62.7 | 17.4 | 16.8 | 34.2 | 3.1 | 100.0 |
| Eighth Plan (1992-1997) | 55.6 | 6.2 | 61.8 | 20.4 | 15.4 | 35.8 | 2.5 | 100.0 |
| Ninth Plan (1997-2002) | 58.7 | 6.0 | 64.7 | 20.0 | 10.6 | 30.6 | 4.9 | 100.0 |
| Tenth Plan (2002-2007) | 53.2 | 8.6 | 61.9 | 20.3 | 11.8 | 32.1 | 6.1 | 100.0 |

*Source*[10]: *State Finances—A Study of Budgets* (various years), Reserve Bank of India Bulletin.

However, the states' devolution needs are still unmet. Although the states' share in total expenditures increased from 52 per cent in 1990-91 to 58 per cent in 2005-06, Rao *et al.* argue that it does not signify an increase in decentralisation. Rather, the spending financed by specific purpose transfer, where the states have little maneuverability, has gone up sharply. A comparison of allocation of grants to local bodies through the last three finance commissions and *inter se* distribution indicates that more than half of the total transfer as recommended by the Tenth FC has gone to large and populous states and their *panchayats* and municipalities.

In the case of the EFC, the criteria of equity, backwardness (index of deprivation), tax effort and the newly constructed index of decentralisation, were adopted for *inter se* distribution but found not very effective. Thus, the EFC ended up with similar inequities with the major share of devolution retained by five states. Lastly, even the TFC could not make any major departure from this trend, although it did manage to give a little more to poorer states thanks to the index of deprivation. As Table 2.6 shows, industrially developed Maharashtra has been earmarked 25.73 per

---

10.   Rao *et al.* (2008).

## Table 2.6

*Shares of States in Twelfth Finance Commission Allocation (2005-2010)*

| Sl.No. | State | Panchayats | | Municipalities | |
|---|---|---|---|---|---|
| | | Per cent | (Rs. crore) | Per cent | (Rs. crore) |
| 1 | Andhra Pradesh | 7.935 | 1587 | 7.480 | 374 |
| 2 | Arunachal Pradesh | 0.340 | 68 | 0.060 | 3 |
| 3 | Assam | 2.630 | 526 | 1.100 | 55 |
| 4 | Bihar | 8.120 | 1624 | 2.840 | 142 |
| 5 | Chhattisgarh | 3.075 | 615 | 1.760 | 88 |
| 6 | Goa | 0.090 | 18 | 0.240 | 12 |
| 7 | Gujarat | 4.655 | 931 | 8.280 | 414 |
| 8 | Haryana | 1.940 | 388 | 1.820 | 91 |
| 9 | Himachal Pradesh | 0.735 | 147 | 0.160 | 8 |
| 10 | Jammu & Kashmir | 1.405 | 281 | 0.760 | 38 |
| 11 | Jharkhand | 2.410 | 482 | 1.960 | 98 |
| 12 | Karnataka | 4.440 | 888 | 6.460 | 323 |
| 13 | Kerala | 4.925 | 985 | 2.980 | 149 |
| 14 | Madhya Pradesh | 8.315 | 1663 | 7.220 | 361 |
| 15 | Maharashtra | 9.915 | 1983 | 15.820 | 791 |
| 16 | Manipur | 0.230 | 46 | 0.180 | 9 |
| 17 | Meghalaya | 0.250 | 50 | 0.160 | 8 |
| 18 | Mizoram | 0.100 | 20 | 0.200 | 10 |
| 19 | Nagaland | 0.200 | 40 | 0.120 | 6 |
| 20 | Orissa | 4.015 | 803 | 2.080 | 104 |
| 21 | Punjab | 1.620 | 324 | 3.420 | 171 |
| 22 | Rajasthan | 6.150 | 1230 | 4.400 | 220 |
| 23 | Sikkim | 0.065 | 13 | 0.020 | 1 |
| 24 | Tamil Nadu | 4.350 | 870 | 11.440 | 572 |
| 25 | Tripura | 0.285 | 57 | 0.160 | 8 |
| 26 | Uttar Pradesh | 14.640 | 2928 | 10.340 | 517 |
| 27 | Uttarakhand | 0.810 | 162 | 0.680 | 34 |
| 28 | West Bengal | 6.355 | 1271 | 7.860 | 393 |
| | | 100.000 | 20000 | 100.00 | 5000 |

cent of the total allocations of Rs. 25,000 crore, followed by underdeveloped Uttar Pradesh at 24.98 per cent. The next three states with the highest share are: Tamil Nadu (15.79 per cent), Madhya Pradesh (15.53 per cent) and Andhra Pradesh (15.41 per cent). In comparison, the bottom three states of Mizoram, Nagaland and Goa have around 0.3 per cent, while Sikkim has got 0.085 per cent.

The Thirteenth Finance Commission therefore must take into account the needs of the states, especially the poorer ones, in meeting basic expenditure in social sectors such as basic education and health care, and help design an incentive system into the transfer formula so as to ensure comparable standards in these services across rural-urban areas and across the country.

## Problems in CFC Funds Release to ULBs

It is also true that state-level administrations are not prompt in devolving CFC resources to the local governments. Further, there is often misuse of funds, most often in the form of diverting funds meant for *panchayats* and ULBs to other areas. Tables 2.7 and 2.8 give an idea of how funds released to local governments have always lagged behind the actual CFC recommendations.

**Table 2.7**

*Central Finance Commission Allocations and Release (in Rs. crore)*

*[Constitutional provisions as per Article 280(3) (bb) and (cc)]*

| Local Governments | 10th CFC (1995-2000) | 11th CFC (2000-2005) | 12th CFC (2005-2010) |
|---|---|---|---|
| PRIs | 4380.93 [per capita basis] | 8000 | 20000 |
| ULBs | 1000 [ratio of slum population to urban population] | 2000 | 5000 |
| Total | 5380.93 | 10000 | 25000 |
| Actual release | 4410.24 | 6601.00 (P) 1751.88 (U) | 9372.71 (P)* 2145.10 (U)* |

*Note:* *As on 15 February 2008.

*Source:* Rai and Bohra, Status of Devolution and State Finance Commissions, and the Ministry of Panchayati Raj.

There are quite a few reasons for this. There is no uniform pattern for funds transfer from Government of India; in fact, the same ministry could adopt different mechanisms. The process is not transparent or predictable, resulting in plenty of cash alternating with cash starvation at the other end. Solutions in the form of creation of special purpose vehicles have often compounded the problem. Also, installing a countrywide efficient and self-monitoring funds transfer mechanism has not been considered part of core reforms nor does the system incentivise efficient expenditure. Thus, there is ample scope for corruption and delay, even before the money reaches the ultimate user, and examples of misspent allocations abound.

**Table 2.8**

*Allocation of CFC Resources to PRIs and ULBs*

| | PRIs | | | | ULBs | | |
| --- | --- | --- | --- | --- | --- | --- | --- |
| *State* | *10th* | *11th* | *12th* | *State* | *10th* | *11th* | *12th* |
| UP | 17.34 | 16.49 | 14.6 | Mah. | 13.3 | 15.8 | 15.8 |
| Bihar | 11.38 | 9.81 | 8.1 | UP | 12.1 | 12.6 | 10.3 |
| AP | 8.01 | 9.5 | 7.9 | WB | 12 | 9.9 | 7.9 |
| MP | 7.96 | 8.9 | 8.3 | TN | 11.6 | 9.7 | 11.4 |
| Mah. | 7.92 | 8.2 | 9.9 | AP | 7.4 | 8.2 | 8.2(Guj.) |
| Total | 52.61 | 52.9 | 48.8 | Total | 56.4 | 56.2 | 53.6 |

*Source:* PRIA (2009).

According to senior officials in the Ministry of Panchayati Raj,[11] 'augmenting' state consolidated funds to 'supplement' *panchayat* resources has not happened. Instead, examples of unlawful diversion of funds abound. Some examples:

- Haryana and Andhra Pradesh diverted EFC grants to State-funded programmes run outside the *panchayats*.

- Karnataka delayed release of funds for nine months after release by the Centre and lost the last instalment following late submission of utilisation certificates.

- UP purchased computers for government offices using EFC funds.

- Arunachal Pradesh used EFC funds to bail out a collapsing cooperative bank and submitted a false utilisation certificate to claim the first instalment of the TFC release, which still was not released to *panchayats* even two years after.

- Odisha used entire TFC funds for the water supply department.

- Kerala does not release any TFC funds to *panchayats*, on the ground that they have subsumed it in the State *panchayat* transfers.

---

11. This section is based on personal interviews conducted in 2008 with T.R. Raghunandan, Joint Secretary, Ministry of Panchayati Raj.

The TFC has tried to streamline the funds transfer process at the states by allocating two equal instalments in July and January every year. States are to mandatorily transfer these grants to the local governments within 15 days of the money being credited to the states' account. They are also to provide a certificate of release within 15 days of the receipt of instalment, certifying date of receipt and date of release to local governments. In case of delayed release, states are penalised and have to pay interest to the RBI. All this allocation, release and expenditure are to be audited by the CAG. A high-level committee headed by the chief secretary and the finance secretary and department secretaries as members are now required to be set up to meet quarterly to monitor the release as well as utilisation of funds and provide details to the Union finance ministry. Of course, it is another matter that even this system is not being efficiently implemented in many states except a few. And there is also a huge opposition to the CAG as well as non-cooperation.

3

# Devolving Neither Money Nor Power

*The Role of SFCs in Strengthening Urban Local Bodies*

The Constitutional Amendments provided an illustrative list of functions appropriate for local government, which included planning for economic and social development, urban poverty alleviation, even urban forestry. Secondly, they limited the degree to which state governments would be able to suspend democratic local government. Finally, and most important, they provided for a revision of state-local fiscal relations at regular interval through mechanism of state finance commission.

Under the new fiscal devolution system/framework every state government is required to constitute, once in five years, a finance commission and entrust it with the task of reviewing the financial position of local governments and making recommendations as to the principles that should govern:

- The distribution between the state and the local governments of the net proceeds of the taxes, duties, tolls and fees that can be levied by the state;

- The determination of the taxes, duties, tolls and fees that may be assigned to or appropriated by the local governments; and

- The grants-in-aid to local governments from the consolidated fund of the state.

Under Articles 243I and 243Y, the SFC is required to review the financial position of *panchayats*/municipalities and recommend to the governor, *inter alia*, the principles of distribution and the shares of proceeds of sharable taxes, duties, tolls and fees between state and *panchayats*/municipalities as well as measures to improve their financial position.

Article 243G states the powers, authority and responsibilities of the *panchayats*. All the 29 subjects are enlisted in the Eleventh Schedule. Article 243W explains the powers, authority and responsibilities of municipalities, the details of 18 subjects listed in the Twelfth Schedule. The second most important component of external sources of revenue for urban or rural local bodies is the devolution of grants by state finance commission and the state government development schemes.

State Finance Commission's recommendations are generally based on the following considerations:

- Financial review of the local bodies for the last six/seven years.

- Recommendations of the previous state finance commission.

- Recommendations of the last two central finance commission.

- State's financial position.

- Existing system of data collection and its maintenance.

- Revenue resource and its demand for next five years.

## SFCs: A Story of Neglect

Almost all the states except three have completed two SFCs and 12 have completed three, though their periods of operation have not been coterminous with the central finance commissions. The first SFC was set up in most states around 1994-1996, except for Arunachal Pradesh, Goa and the new states formed in 2000. The second finance commissions were constituted during the years 1998-2000 for a period ranging from 2000 to 2008. A few states which were prompt with their second SFC reports managed to set up a third. Annexure I, Tables A-1.2 and A-1.3 give the details of the timelines of the formation of the SFCs, report submission and action taken.

The new fiscal devolution system introduced by the Eleventh Finance Commission brought about a major change in the scope of the tasks of the central finance commission. Article 280(3) requires the CFC to suggest measures to increase the consolidated fund of a state to supplement the resources of the local governments on the basis of the recommendations made by the SFC. Thus, it makes the SFC the only channel to address issues of state-local fiscal relations and places on it a unique role in fiscal decentralisation and local finance issues.[1]

State governments, feels Dr. Chakravarthy Rangarajan, former chair of the TFC and former RBI governor, have not paid serious attention to SFCs.[2] His contention would be right. As Table 3.1 shows, not only have all states been unable to complete three rounds of SFC, some states, such as Chhattisgarh, have just managed to complete one SFC even though, being born in 2000, it had enough time for two.

**Table 3.1**

*Status of SFCs and their Reports in Major States*

| No. | State | 1st SFC | 2nd SFC | 3rd SFC |
|---|---|---|---|---|
| 1 | Andhra Pradesh | Y | Y | Y |
| 2 | Assam | Y | Y | Y |
| 3 | Chhattisgarh | Y | | |
| 4 | Gujarat | Y | Y | |
| 5 | Haryana | Y | Y | Y |
| 6 | Himachal Pradesh | Y | Y | Y |
| 7 | Karnataka | Y | Y | Y |
| 8 | Kerala | Y | Y | Y |
| 9 | Madhya Pradesh | Y | Y | Y |
| 10 | Maharashtra | Y | Y | |
| 11 | Manipur | Y | Y | |
| 12 | Odisha | Y | Y | |
| 13 | Punjab | Y | Y | Y |
| 14 | Rajasthan | Y | Y | Y |
| 15 | Sikkim | Y | | |
| 16 | Tamil Nadu | Y | Y | Y |
| 17 | Tripura | Y | | |
| 18 | Uttarakhand | Y | Y | |
| 19 | Uttar Pradesh | Y | Y | Y |
| 20 | West Bengal | Y | Y | Y |
| | Total states | 20 | 17 | 12 |

There is wide variation among states in devolution of funds, functions and functionaries, as well as implementation of the SFC recommendations.

---

1. Joshi (2005).

2. Speech at National Seminar on *Status of State Finance Commissions* organised by PRIA and RGCIS, December 2, 2005.

- While amending the Municipal Acts, most of the states included the list of functions in the 12th Schedule automatically, without reviewing as they were supposed to do. Only a few states have carried out a comprehensive review; these are Kerala, West Bengal and Tamil Nadu which have transferred these responsibilities to the ULBs. These states have not restricted themselves to the Twelfth Schedule but also devolved some additional functions to the ULBs.

- Whereas Bihar, Gujarat, Himachal Pradesh, Manipur, Punjab, Rajasthan and Haryana have included all the functions as enlisted in the Twelfth Schedule in their amended state municipal laws, Andhra Pradesh has not made any changes in the existing list of municipal functions.

- The states of Karnataka, Kerala, Madhya Pradesh, Maharashtra, Odisha, Tamil Nadu, Uttar Pradesh and West Bengal have amended their municipal laws and added some of the additional functions in the list of municipal functions as suggested in the Twelfth Schedule. There is a lot of difference in the assignment of obligatory and discretionary functions to the municipal bodies among the states.[3] Whereas functions like planning for the social and economic development, urban forestry and protection of the environment and promotion of ecological aspects are obligatory functions for the municipalities of Maharashtra, in Karnataka these are discretionary functions.

- Rajasthan was the first state to constitute an SFC and is among only 12 states to have set up the third.

Clearly, though SFCs are the vehicle to ensure percolation of democracy right down to the grassroots, the states show a reluctance in not only setting them up but also accepting their recommendations readily. In some states, the delay in setting up an SFC, getting it to submit a report and then take action over it has involved up to four years, while only a handful of states have managed to do it in two years. Such a huge delay in the implementation of SFC recommendations not only slows down the process of fiscal decentralisation but also defeats the very purpose of sourcing the much-needed funds for local governments.

This has also resulted in the synchronisation problem, with the SFCs being set up at times that are very different from the CFCs' tenure, making

---

3.   Mathur (1999).

it tough for each to take into account the recommendations of the other. As per the ToR, the CFC has to give its recommendation regarding the devolution of resources to local bodies based on the assessment made by the SFCs. The CFCs till now have not used the requirements of local bodies recommended by the SFCs on account of heterogeneity in their approach and the different award period.

At the state level, there are two problems: one is about the timely implementation of SFC recommendations as per the action taken reports (ATR), which is enormously delayed by the state government. The second one pertains to the acceptance of major recommendations with respect to devolution of resources. Often, the SFC recommendations may be partially or fully rejected by the state government and sometimes they are. Ideally, states should accept at least the major recommendations made by the SFC and implement them in a particular timeframe as well, which does not always happen.

In fact, the second SFC of Andhra Pradesh has bemoaned the fact[4] that the recommendations of the first SFC, its predecessor, were not accepted in full by the state. Out of 84 recommendations, 24 were not accepted, 5 were accepted partially, with no reason given for the non-acceptance and some recommendations were accepted but no follow-up action was taken. The first SFC had recommended devolution of Rs. 979.16 crore every year for the local bodies, but only a much lower figure of Rs. 434.42 crore was accepted. Some grants were initially not accepted by the government but were subsequently accepted after pressure from *panchayat sarpanches.*

## Transfer of Resources under State Finance Commissions

As we have said before, the SFC has to recommend the devolution of grants from taxes, duties, toll and fees. While making the recommendations, some states have gone for global sharing of tax revenue, whereas some states have recommended for devolution of resources from both tax and non-tax sources. Some states are still continuing with specific sharing of individual taxes. We try to summarise the SFC recommendations in the area of resources allocation in Table 3.2.

---

4.  Mishra (n.d.)

### Box 3.1

*TFC Recommendations on Working of SFCs*

*Para 8.55*

i. The states should avoid delays in the constitution of the SFCs, their constitution in phases, frequent reconstitution, submission of reports and tabling of the ATR in the legislature. It is desirable that SFCs are constituted at least two years before the required date of submission of their recommendations, and the deadline should be so decided as to allow the state government at least three months' time for tabling the ATR, preferably along with the budget for the ensuing financial year.

ii. The SFC reports should be readily available to the central finance commission, when the latter is constituted so that an assessment of the state's need could be made by the central finance commission on the basis of uniform principles. This requires that these reports should not be too dated. As the periodicity of constitution of the central finance commission is predictable, the states should time the constitution of their SFCs suitably.

iii. SFCs must be constituted with people of eminence and competence with qualification and experience in the relevant fields.

iv. The convention established at the national level of accepting the principal recommendations of the finance commission without modification, should be followed at the state level in respect of SFC reports.

v. The SFCs must clearly identify the issues which require action on the part of the Central government to augment the consolidated fund of the state and list them out in a separate chapter for the consideration of the central finance commission.

vi. The suggestion made by SFCs regarding raising the ceiling on professional tax is endorsed for action by Central government.

vii. It is desirable that the SFCs follow the procedure adopted by the central finance commission for transfer of resources from the Centre to the states in respect of resource transfers from state governments to local bodies. The SFC reports should contain an estimation and analysis of the finances of the state government as well as the local bodies at the pre- and post-transfer stages along with a quantification of the revenues that could be generated additionally by the local bodies by adopting the measures recommended therein. The gaps that may still remain would then constitute the basis for the measures to be recommended by the Central Finance Commission.

viii. While estimating the resources of the local bodies, the SFCs should follow a normative approach in the assessment of revenues and expenditure rather than make forecasts based on historical trends.

ix. A permanent SFC cell may be created in the finance department of state governments as the collection and collation of data would need to be done constantly and data would need to be made available to the SFC.

## Table 3.2

*Devolution of Resources through 1st, 2nd and 3rd SFCs*

### A. Global Sharing of Total Revenue (Tax and Non-Tax Sources)

| 1ˢᵗ SFC | | 2ⁿᵈ SFC | | 3ʳᵈ SFC | |
|---|---|---|---|---|---|
| *State* | *% Share* | *State* | *% Share* | *State* | *% Share* |
| Andhra Pradesh | 39.2 | Andhra Pradesh | 4.9 | Himachal Pradesh | 1.41 |
| Karnataka | 36.0 | Gujarat | 31.15 | Kerala | 25 |
| Kerala | 1.0 | Karnataka | 40 | | |
| Madhya Pradesh | 2.91 | Kerala | 3.5 | | |
| Uttarakhand | 11.0 | Odisha | 10 | | |
| | | Uttarakhand | 10 | | |

### B. Global Sharing of Tax Revenue

| 1ˢᵗ SFC | | 2ⁿᵈ SFC | | 3ʳᵈ SFC | |
|---|---|---|---|---|---|
| *State* | *% Share* | *State* | *% Share* | *State* | *% share* |
| Assam | 2.0 | Assam | 3.5 | Punjab | 4.0 |
| Punjab | 20.0 | Madhya Pradesh | 4.0 | Rajasthan | 3.5 |
| Rajasthan | 2.2 | Maharashtra | 8.0 | Tamil Nadu | 9.0 |
| Tamil Nadu | 8.0 | Punjab | 4.0 | | |
| Uttar Pradesh | 7.0 | Rajasthan | 2.3 | | |
| West Bengal | 16.0 | Tamil Nadu | 8.0 | | |
| | | Uttar Pradesh | 12.5 | | |
| | | West Bengal | 16.0 | | |

### C. Sharing of Individual Taxes

**1ˢᵗ SFC**

| | |
|---|---|
| Gujarat | (i) 20% of MVT (motor vehicle tax stamp) |
| | (ii) 50% of entertainment tax & show tax |
| | (iii) 10% of royalty on minor minerals |
| | (iv) 5 paise per unit tax on electricity consumption |
| Maharashtra | (i) 25% to 100% of entertainment tax collected in municipal limit |
| | (ii) 25% of vehicle tax |
| | (iii) 10% of profession tax |

**2ⁿᵈ SFC**

| | |
|---|---|
| Haryana | (i) 50% of net income of ent. tax |
| | (ii) 10% of show tax-entire proceeds |
| | (iii) 20% of net proceeds from vehicle tax |
| | (iv) 5 paise per unit tax on electricity consumption |
| | (v) 10% of income from royalty on minor minerals |
| | (vi) 35% of net proceeds from local area development tax (LADT) |

### D. Devolution of Fixed Amount/Grants

**1ˢᵗ SFC**

| | |
|---|---|
| Himachal Pradesh | An amount equal to Rs. 12.2 crore as grants in lieu of octroi |

**2ˢᵗ SFC**

| | |
|---|---|
| Himachal Pradesh | An amount equal to Rs. 19.66 crore as grants to ULBs |

Post implementation of the recommendations of the SFCs, there has been a drastic change in the structure and methods of state transfers in many states. Transfers are high or low depending on their revenue raising powers and the expenditure needs.[5] Mathur says, "Many of the transfers are not possible to be separately accounted for, as these are absorbed directly into state government expenditures."[6] A systematic evaluation of the fiscal transfer between state and urban local bodies has not been made.

**Table 3.3**

*Some Major Recommendations of State Finance Commissions*

| No. | Name of the State | Recommendations |
|---|---|---|
| 1. | Andhra Pradesh | • 10.93 per cent of the tax and non-tax revenue of the state (*panchayats* 9.14 per cent and municipalities 1.79 per cent) to devolve additionally on rural and urban bodies. |
| | | • Increase of per capita grant; GPs- 1:4, MPs- 5:8 and ZPs-2:4. |
| 2. | Gujarat | • *Gram panchayats* mandated to levy property tax, water tax and conservancy tax. |
| | | • Land revenue distribution to be based on the average of last three years. |
| | | • Panchayat finance board with an independent status to be re-constituted. |
| | | • A share of professional tax should be given to *panchayats*. |
| 3. | Haryana | • Devolution of 20 per cent of royalty on minor minerals to *gram panchayats* and urban local bodies. |
| | | • 7.5 per cent of net receipts on stamps duty and registration fees to devolve on Panchayati Raj bodies and the amount distributed district-wise for 'Decentralised Planning' schemes. |
| | | • Levy of Haryana Rural Development Fund to be increased from 1 per cent to 2 per cent. |
| | | • Incentive grants in the form of cash award for the three best performing *panchayats* at the district, block and village level. |
| 4. | Himachal Pradesh | • A Rural Infrastructure Maintenance Corpus to be set up for maintaining already created rural assets, *viz.*, primary schools, health centres, veterinary dispensaries etc. |
| | | • *Gram panchayats* and *panchayat samitis* to be provided with Rs. 1395.47 lakh and Rs. 63.39 lakh respectively for the payment of honoraria and office expenses. |

contd...

---

5.  Thakur (2006).

6.  Mathur (2006).

*...contd...*

| No. | Name of the State | Recommendations |
|-----|-------------------|-----------------|
| 5. | Karnataka | • Devolution of finances in percentage terms and not in absolute terms.<br>• Transferring 36 per cent of the state government's total non-loan gross revenue receipts in the ratio of 85 per cent to *panchayats* and 15 per cent to municipalities.<br>• Five indicators for devolving finances: population (33.33 per cent); area (33.33 per cent); illiteracy rate (11.11 per cent); number of persons per hospital bed (11.12 per cent); and road length per sq km (11.12 per cent).<br>• Share of each tier: 25 per cent for *gram panchayat*, 35 per cent for *taluka* (block) *panchayat*, and 40 per cent for *zilla* (district) *panchayat*. |
| 6. | Kerala | • Vehicle tax compensation, which could be up to 25 per cent of net collection of motor vehicle tax, to be distributed among local bodies.<br>• Proceeds of building tax to be assigned to *gram panchayats* and municipalities.<br>• Earmarking a portion of the income from the sale of court fee stamps to local bodies.<br>• State revenue to be allocated in the ratio of 15 per cent to *taluka panchayats* and 70 per cent to *gram panchayats*. |
| 7. | Madhya Pradesh | • Grants to *gram panchayats* to discharge basic functions<br>• PRIs to be paid 2.5 per cent of the total provision for sponsored programmes as agents' grant-in-aid.<br>• A general-purpose grant of Rs. 14.65 crore and Rs. 1.5 crore to be given to *zilla* and *janpad* (town) *panchayats* respectively for 1995-96, with an annual increase of 10 per cent.<br>• One-time non-recurring grant for furnishing and maintaining the PRI offices.<br>• Devolution criteria for municipalities—15 per cent in proportion to SC/ST population and 85 per cent based on population, area, agricultural labour, per hectare gross value of agricultural output, number of workers in registered factories per lakh of population, per capita consumption of electricity, and literacy rate. For *gram panchayats*, it is 75 per cent based on population and 25 per cent on area. |
| 8. | Maharashtra | • 10 per cent of the total recovery by government from profession tax to be given to local bodies.<br>• Government payment of grant of land revenue and cess to local bodies to be linked to demand and not actual recovery.<br>• PRIs to be given 66.67 per cent of the demand of land revenue and cess as a grant in advance every year. |

*contd...*

*...contd...*

| No. | Name of the State | Recommendations |
|---|---|---|
| 9. | Assam | • Share of state taxes for transfer to local bodies to be 2 per cent every year.<br>• Reform property tax through tax mapping and record keeping, change in method assessment, periodic review in assessment, simplification of procedures.<br>• Transfer of 10 per cent of the net proceeds of motor vehicle tax. |
| 10. | Tripura | • 10 per cent of the state's share of central tax to *zilla panchayats*, 8 per cent to *panchayat samiti* and 2 per cent to *gram panchayats*.<br>• *Panchayats* to get 50 per cent of the revenue earned from sales tax, additional tax, purchase tax and luxury tax in the ratio of 30 per cent to *gram panchayats*, 15 per cent to *panchayat samiti* and 5 per cent to *zilla parishads*.<br>• 32 per cent of the collection from agricultural income and land revenue to be passed on to the intermediate tier at uniform rate of 2 per cent per *samiti*. |
| 11. | Odisha | • Massive external assistance to local bodies to upgrade basic civil services.<br>• Surcharge on stamp duty for transfer of properties in rural areas. |
| 12. | Punjab | • Assignment of land revenue to *gram panchayats*.<br>• State to share 20 per cent of the net proceeds of stamp duty, motor vehicle tax, electricity duty and entertainment tax with *panchayats* and municipalities. |
| 13. | Rajasthan | • 2.18 per cent of the net proceeds of all state taxes (to be placed in a divisible pool) to be devolved on PRIs and urban local bodies in the ratio of 3:4:1.<br>• Set up a finance corporation in rural and urban areas.<br>• *Panchayats* to make matching contributions to get the assistance for most centrally sponsored schemes.<br>• Government grant-in-aid to *panchayats* be raised from Rs. 5 to Rs. 11 per head (1995-96). |
| 14. | Tamil Nadu | • Local cess surcharge on stamp duty assigned to *panchayats*.<br>• 15 per cent of resource devolution to be reserved as 'equalisation and incentive fund' and shared between *panchayats* and municipalities at the ratio of 60:40. Criteria for distribution of funds—population (50 per cent), SC/ST population (15 per cent), per capita house tax collection (15 per cent), core civil services/ infrastructure maintenance deficiencies (20 per cent).<br>• Revision of house tax every third year based on plinth area rental value. |

*contd...*

*...contd...*

| No. | Name of the State | Recommendations |
|---|---|---|
| 15. | Uttar Pradesh | • *Panchayats* to be given 3 per cent of net state tax revenue for a five-year period starting from 1996. |
| | | • Surcharge on land revenue to be charged at the rate of 50 per cent of land revenue and to be collected by the state revenue department along with the land revenue. |
| | | • All *zilla panchayats* to levy circumstances and property tax. |
| 16. | West Bengal | • Sharing of 16 per cent of the net proceeds of all the taxes collected by the state government with *panchayats* and municipalities. |
| | | • Proportional allocation of state revenue between *panchayats* at the ratio of 30 per cent to *zilla panchayats*, 20 per cent to *taluka panchayat samitis* and 50 per cent to *gram panchayats*. |

---

**Box 3.2**

*SFCs and Devolution: The Points of Concern*

- Non-synchronisation of SFC and CFC tenures and reports should end—the last three CFCs could not make use of reports of SFCs.

- CFCs could not arrive at their own estimate of resource gaps and resorted to ad hoc allocations for local bodies.

- Most SFCs failed to emphasise the link between revenue-raising and expenditure responsibilities, a link that is needed to induce fiscal responsibility.

- SFCs recommended a number of grants for local bodies some of which are ad hoc and promoted dependence.

- Local bodies have limited powers to raise resources and taxes and duties collected by them are not very elastic or buoyant, so taxation powers should be strengthened.

- Vertical imbalance, fiscal dependence and borrowing constraints and limits affect the functioning of local bodies, so functional devolution should be made effectively.

- Devolution of functions, fund and functionaries should be based on activity mapping as agreed at the round table conference of ministers in 2004.

- A body of SFCs must look into and formulate guidelines on the ToRs for SFCs as laid out in the Constitution, the composition of SFC as also a standard for quality and findings of the report.

- Improve the base of municipal finance statistics (MFS) and promote nationwide use of standardised formats for municipal accounts.

# 4 | Handicapped by Birth
## *Weak Revenues and Fiscal Dependence of Municipal Bodies*

The acid test of the strength of a municipal government is its capability to generate its domestic source of income namely, tax and non-tax source. Municipalities can levy taxes on lands and buildings, charged as property tax (entry 49), the entry of goods into a local area for consumption, use or sale therein, such as entry tax/octroi (entry 52), on consumption and sale of electricity, or electricity tax (entry 53), on advertisements other than advertisements published in the newspapers and advertisements broadcast by radio or television (entry 55), on animals and boats (entry 58), tolls (entry 59), on professions, trades, callings and employment called professional tax (entry 60), on luxuries, including taxes on entertainment, amusements, betting and gambling, also called luxury and entertainment tax (entry 62) and Fees in respect of any of the matters in the state list (entry 66). Of course, few states levy all these taxes. The first two taxes, especially entry tax/octroi, have traditionally formed the backbone of the revenue income of municipalities.

Non-tax receipts include fees and fines, rates and rents, income from municipal undertakings, user charges and income from municipal investments etc. (entry 66). The Constitution of India does not lay down the revenue base for municipalities; on the contrary, the state governments decide everything such as fixing the authority and base, setting the rate, and even the grants-in-aid and other forms of transfers. Figure 4.1 gives the overall fiscal resource transfer system in India to the local bodies.

**Figure 4.1**

*Formula-Based and Discretionary Fiscal Devolution/Transfers*

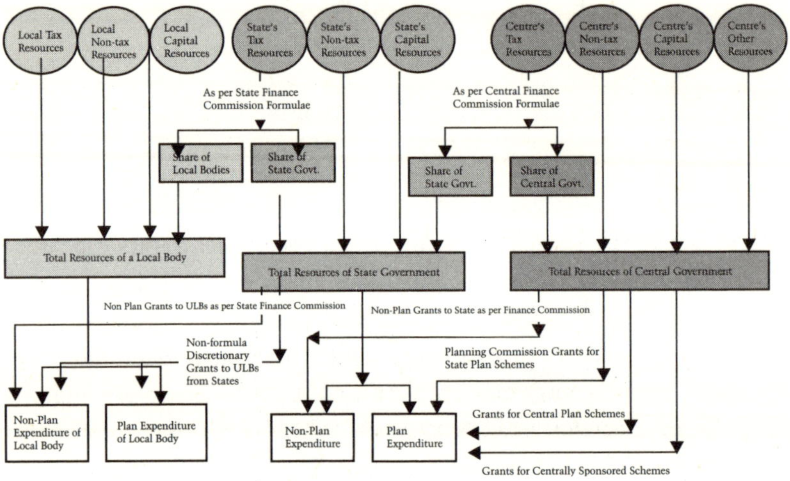

*Source:* Joshi, Ravikant (2005). *Decentralisation and Local Finance Issues.*[1]

# Local Bodies Handicapped in Raising Revenue

The 1992 amendments notwithstanding, local bodies in India remain handicapped in collecting revenue income or widening its base, constraining their essential expenditure. Quoting a study done for the EFC, the TFC pointed out[2] that internal revenue mobilisation by the Panchayati Raj institutions constituted only 4.17 per cent of their total revenue. A report[3] on the finances of *gram panchayats* in Himachal Pradesh for 2005-06 reveals that "the income from the tax revenue (tax, fees, fines rent etc.) of Gram Panchayats in the state constitute a negligible 8.5 per cent of the total receipts of the Panchayat. Similarly, 97 per cent of the Gram Panchayats spends no money on providing civic amenities like sanitation/ street lighting etc."

---

1. Joshi (2005).

2. Report of the TFC, p. 138.

3. Scheme for availing incentive against the net fresh additional resource mobilisation by *Gram Panchayats*, Ministry of Panchayati Raj, Government of Himachal Pradesh, August 2008.

According to a study made by the National Institute for Rural Development for the Twelfth Finance Commission (TFC), there has been a phenomenal dependence of *panchayats* on revenue transfer from both the Union and the state governments. The situation of municipalities could be worse, especially in India's small and medium towns. Mathur and Thakur's study pointed to a very high level of dependence of all types of urban local governments on transfers and grant-in-aids from state governments. Table 4.1 shows the examples of *panchayats*, to make the larger point that such grants are not only discretionary but also difficult to estimate as these are often directly absorbed into state government expenditures.

**Table 4.1**

*State-wise Revenue Composition of Panchayats*
*(As Percentage of Total Revenue) (2002-03)*

| Own Revenue | State | Own Revenue | Other Revenue |
|---|---|---|---|
| Less than 5% | Karnataka | 1.38 | 98.62 |
| | Rajasthan | 2.08 | 97.92 |
| | Gujarat | 2.12 | 97.88 |
| | Bihar | 2.25 | 97.75 |
| | Odisha | 2.93 | 97.07 |
| | Andhra Pradesh | 3.73 | 96.27 |
| Average | All states | 6.84 | 93.16 |
| 5 to 10 per cent | Tamil Nadu | 7.35 | 92.65 |
| | Maharashtra | 8.81 | 91.19 |
| | Uttarakhand | 9.94 | 90.06 |
| | Uttar Pradesh | 10.14 | 89.86 |
| 10 to 25 per cent | Himachal Pradesh | 13.88 | 86.12 |
| | West Bengal | 17.64 | 82.36 |
| | Chhattisgarh | 20.61 | 79.39 |
| | Haryana | 20.82 | 79.18 |
| Above 25 per cent | Kerala | 23.53 | 76.47 |
| | Goa | 28.35 | 71.65 |
| | Madhya Pradesh | 36.53 | 63.47 |
| | Punjab | 55.32 | 44.68 |

*Source:* PRIA.

The National Institute of Public Finance and Policy (NIPFP) study[4] for 23 states observed that though municipal finance statistics were fragile and inadequate and did not allow a logical interpretation of data, the size of municipal sector, measured in terms of what the municipalities raised and spent, was 1 per cent of GDP with large inter-state disparities. The local governments generated much less than 1 per cent (0.63 per cent) of the combined GSDP for 2001-02. Among the states, it varied between the highest levels of 2.16 per cent of GSDP in Maharashtra to 0.07 per cent of GSDP in Bihar. The ratio of municipal own revenues to GSDP is less than 0.40 in all the states except Andhra Pradesh, Gujarat, Karnataka, Maharashtra, Punjab and Tamil Nadu, which shows up the extremely weak link between municipalities and states' economies.

Over a five-year period of 1997-98 to 2001-02, the size of the municipal sector has registered a marginal expansion, both in terms of its share in the total publicly-raised revenues and combined GSDP. In 2001-2002, the size of the municipal sector measured in terms of revenues (what the municipalities generated by way of levy of taxes, duties, fees and fines) was estimated at Rs. 12,748 crore (adjusted for population of all states). Compared to 2.84 per cent in 1997-98, these revenues formed 3.07 per cent of publicly-raised resources, the shares of the Central government and all state governments combined being 57.5 per cent and 39.5 per cent respectively. Nominally, municipal own revenues have risen at an annual average rate of 10.32 per cent.

### Table 4.2

*How Significant are Municipal Revenues*

| Year | Municipalities Own Revenue (Rs. Crore) | Per cent of GDP | Relative Shares of Own Revenues (%) | | |
|---|---|---|---|---|---|
| | | | Municipalities | State Govts. | Central Govts. |
| 1997-98 | 8,434.9 | 0.61 | 2.84 | 33.4 | 63.8 |
| 1998-99 | 9,451.7 | 0.59 | 2.97 | 34.3 | 62.7 |
| 1999-2000 | 10,372.7 | 0.59 | 2.80 | 34.4 | 62.8 |
| 2000-01 | 12,018.4 | 0.63 | 2.98 | 35.1 | 61.9 |
| 2001-02 | 12,7481 | - | 3.07 | 39.5 | 57.5 |

*Note:* Figure for municipal own revenues are adjusted to reflect the revenues for all statutory towns and cities.

*Source:* Mathur and Thakur (2004).

---

4.  The Report of the Twelfth Finance Commission, Chapter 8 on Local Bodies.

Over 1998-99 to 2002-03, per capita own tax revenue was on average Rs. 18.17 in Rajasthan, compared to the state average (15 major states) of Rs. 263.91. While it was growing at 7.6 per cent in the states, compared to 8.3 per cent for per capita own revenue, it actually fell 26.6 per cent in Rajasthan. However, with severe transfer dependence, Rajasthan's per capita own revenue came to a much higher Rs. 123.42, compared to the 15-state average of Rs. 260.06.

The share of own revenue in the total municipal income is low due to total lack of autonomy of municipalities in setting tax rates as well as poor administration, management and collection procedures. The negligible share of local own source revenue (tax and non-tax) is highlighted by Mathur in his paper[5] on "Decentralisation in India: A Report Card" as well as in the NIPFP study. Low proportion of own revenue of the municipalities shows that the own fiscal base of larger towns has weakened and their dependence on external sources has increased.

Transfers to local bodies are justified because the entire nation has a stake in the development of local bodies as they have functions which are not only vital for improving the living conditions of the people but their benefits also spill over beyond the boundaries of local bodies. Ideally, the basic principle governing SFC transfers through fiscal packages should be that the packages would be adequate enough to meet as much of the revenue gap as possible, especially if that gap is owing to the mismatch between their expenditure commitments and their own source revenue due to fiscal disabilities. As C. Rangarajan says, "a good transfer system must establish an appropriate balance between equity and efficiency, a system in which fiscal disadvantage is taken care of, but fiscal imprudence is effectively discouraged."[6]

However, the SFC recommendations and the devolution framework suggested by them so far have failed to cause any perceptible change in the finances of urban local governments. Even 10 years after the 1992 amendment, state governments are sharing less than 5 per cent of their resources with the local governments. Table 4.3 shows that the transfers made by all the states to urban local bodies as per SFC reports or under

5. UMP-Asia *Occasional Paper* No. 47 – July 2000.
6. Rangarajan (2004).

other devolution framework on an average amounted to only 4.47 per cent of state's own revenues during 1997-98 to 2000-01.

**Table 4.3**

*Transfers as a Percentage of State's Own Revenues*

| States | 1997/98 | 1998/99 | 1999/2000 | 2000/01 |
|---|---|---|---|---|
| Andhra Pradesh | 2.91 | 3.88 | 3.91 | 3.08 |
| Assam | 0.66 | 0.53 | 0.48 | 0.66 |
| Bihar | 3.96 | 3.37 | 4.37 | 2.39 |
| Chhattisgarh | - | - | - | 10.83 |
| Goa | 1 | 0.76 | - | 0.67 |
| Gujarat | 1.99 | 2.14 | 2.62 | 2.8 |
| Haryana | 1.13 | 0.69 | 1.4 | 1.74 |
| Karnataka | 2.69 | 3.62 | 4.06 | 4.49 |
| Kerala | 3.17 | 3.74 | 3.65 | 2.58 |
| Madhya Pradesh | 6.78 | 8.28 | 8.76 | 8.13 |
| Maharashtra | 2.19 | 2.21 | 3.35 | 2.82 |
| Odisha | 1.68 | 2.01 | 3.14 | 2.73 |
| Punjab | 1.07 | 1.91 | 1.25 | 1.27 |
| Rajasthan | 2.25 | 5.91 | 6.48 | 6.53 |
| Tamil Nadu | 7.77 | 8.08 | 6.85 | 6.05 |
| Uttarakhand | - | - | - | 14.24 |
| Uttar Pradesh | 5.26 | 7.26 | 6.21 | 5.52 |
| West Bengal | 9.01 | 10.37 | 15.25 | 11.95 |
| Average, all states | 3.76 | 4.52 | 4.93 | 4.47 |

*Source:* Mathur and Thakur (2004).

The proportion of state resources transferred to the local bodies was only 2 per cent in Rajasthan, which ranked 15th among states.

Similarly, even the grants-in-aid provided by the CFCs from the resources of Union governments have had a negligible impact on the finances of urban local governments. Table 4.4 shows that the Eleventh FC grant of Rs. 400 crore came to a mere 3.35 per cent of own municipal revenues.

Absence of predictability and stability in the level of transfer is one of the most significant weaknesses of the existing transfers system in India.[7] Transfers to municipalities make up 3.85 per cent of the combined own

---

7.   NIUA (1997).

resources of states. Between 1997-98 and 2001-02, these have risen by only 0.54 percentage points, say Mathur and Thakur. Even such a small rise has put additional strain on the finances of state governments. Yet, the SFCs have preferred to maintain the status quo and refrained from examining inter-governmental fiscal relations with reference to the 1992 amendment.

**Table 4.4**

*Municipal Own Revenue in 2001-02 and Distribution
of Finance Commission Grant (Rs. Lakh)*

| *States* | *Municipal Own Revenue* | *Municipal Share of Grant (Rs. 40,000 lakh)* | *EFC Grant as Percentage of Own Revenue* |
| --- | --- | --- | --- |
| | *(Rs. lakh)* | *(Rs. lakh)* | *(per cent)* |
| Andhra Pradesh | 71745.71 | 3293.20 | 4.59 |
| Assam | 3825.81 | 430.80 | 11.26 |
| Bihar | 3408.44 | 1878.00 | 32.61 |
| Chhattisgarh | 11599.83 | - | - |
| Goa | 1858.772 | 92.80 | 4.99 |
| Gujarat | 144849.22 | 2650.40 | 1.83 |
| Haryana | 12106.95 | 732.80 | 6.05 |
| Himachal Pradesh | 1978.93 | 78.00 | 3.94 |
| Jammu & Kashmir | 1199.02 | 313.20 | 26.12 |
| Jharkhand | 2351.23 | | |
| Karnataka | 53448.98 | 2496.40 | 4.67 |
| Kerala | 22432.79 | 1504.80 | 6.71 |
| Madhya Pradesh | 29437.00 | 3120.40 | 7.60 |
| Maharashtra | 587058.29 | 6325.20 | 1.08 |
| Odisha | 10176.83 | 799.20 | 7.85 |
| Punjab | 68551.18 | 1094.40 | 1.60 |
| Rajasthan | 10339.68 | 1988.40 | 19.23 |
| Tamil Nadu | 88079.00 | 3867.20 | 4.39 |
| Uttarakhand | 2320.61 | - | - |
| Uttar Pradesh | 26551.00 | 5032.80 | 17.43 |
| West Bengal | 442201.69 | 3949.60 | 9.36 |
| Arunachal Pradesh | - | 136.00 | - |
| Manipur | - | 88.00 | - |
| Meghalaya | - | 776.80 | - |
| Mizoram | - | 35.60 | - |
| Nagaland | - | 4.00 | - |
| Sikkim | - | | - |
| All states total/average | 1195520.92 | 40000.00 | 3.35 |

*Source:* Mathur and Thakur (2004).

The financial dependence of the municipalities on state transfers puts the state governments in a position of absolute power over urban local governments, tends to subvert democratic decentralisation and generates high levels of frustration in municipal officers. Over time, the municipal revenue bases have been eroded by withdrawal of taxes that they were previously entitled to collect. A glaring example is the octroi tax, which was a very rich source of revenue to municipal bodies. Its abolition significantly eroded the financial strength of the municipal bodies and the compensation they received did not have the buoyancy that the tax had. Another unfortunate example is the recent abolition of the *tehbazari* tax/charge in Uttar Pradesh, which was a good source of revenue, especially for the small and medium towns, which are market hubs for agricultural and other primary products. Concomitantly, the era of decentralisation has brought them more responsibility.

Also, the municipal tax portfolio has inherent constraints. Conventional sources such as property tax, tax on professions, tax on vehicles and the like, and user charges and fees are not only meagre but less productive and buoyant too. They are not updated with the passage of time; property tax reforms are only now being undertaken in some cities. Also wealth-based taxes, unlike income-based taxes, are inelastic as they are not connected to people's ability to pay and therefore suffer from strong resistance from the taxpayers. Even user charges face similar resistance as these are related to basic urban necessities and come through as a matter of right to users.

Municipal bodies in Bihar have an annual per capita revenue generation of Rs. 39.5 compared to Rs. 1493 by those in Maharashtra. Maharashtra, with a 14.4 per cent share in the total urban population of the country, accounted for 48.5 per cent of the revenues generated by all municipal bodies. Including Gujarat, with an urban population share of 7.13 per cent and revenues share of 11.97 per cent and Punjab, with a population share of 3.22 per cent and revenues share of 6.23 per cent, then, only three states of India generate resources more than their share in the population. Municipal bodies of only four states—Goa, Gujarat, Maharashtra and Punjab—have per capita own revenue averages above the national average of Rs. 482 per capita.

Measured by per capita municipal own revenues and annual growth rate, the best states were found to be Punjab, Karnataka, Goa and Andhra Pradesh. At the bottom are Haryana, Madhya Pradesh, Odisha and Rajasthan. Despite high growth rates, Gujarat and Tamil Nadu score low in municipal revenues.

Performance of municipalities on both revenue mobilisation and spending levels vary across states. States with high per capita income were also the ones taking major reform initiatives and were better performing. Based on the studies commissioned and the SFC reports, the TFC estimated the uncovered gap of the local bodies at a whopping Rs. 74,000 crore over a five-year period and managed to allocate only Rs. 25,000 crore, leaving a huge deficit.

In 2001-02, the share of transfers in the revenues of municipalities was 31.7 per cent on an average. But the level of dependence varied. In Karnataka, according to the second SFC, municipal corporations were dependent on state devolution to the extent of 60 per cent, while it was 65 per cent in Andhra Pradesh. In fact, several municipalities in states all across the country are almost entirely transfer-dependent for running local services. There are the historically transfer-dependent municipalities in states such as Bihar, Himachal Pradesh, Jammu & Kashmir, Uttar Pradesh, West Bengal and Tripura. The dependence of urban local bodies was as high as 83.71 per cent in case of Jammu & Kashmir, 83.33 per cent in case of Rajasthan and 74.48 per cent in Uttar Pradesh. Then there are municipalities whose dependence on transfers is growing and they are found in states such as Haryana, Odisha and Rajasthan. The third category is of municipalities in states which have recently abolished octroi and therefore gotten to depend on transfers, such as Gujarat and Maharashtra. Unfortunately, this increasing dependence has not been accompanied by a corresponding transfer of fiscal powers.

What explains such large variation in the performance of municipalities in the different states? Is the variation dependent on factors endogenous to the municipal system or exogenous and to what extent? Part of the answer lies in the fact that there are large inter-state differences in the functional and fiscal domain of municipalities. Based on that, municipal bodies could be crudely fashioned into three groups: (a) those that have a comparatively larger functional and an equally large fiscal domain; (b) those that have a comparatively larger functional domain, but a narrower fiscal base; and (c) those that have a larger fiscal domain but a narrower functional jurisdiction. This fact would explain, in a significant way, why the levels of revenue incomes and expenditures are high in Gujarat and Maharashtra and low in other states. Likewise, they have access to octroi which provide to the municipal corporations in these states, large revenues, enabling them to run these services.

## Revenue Situation in Small and Medium Towns

It is the poor performance of municipal bodies in small and medium towns that drags down the average municipal revenues in India; the larger towns are doing rather well actually. This is clear from the RBI study[8] of primary data obtained from budget documents of 35 major municipal corporations (for cities with a population of more than a million) for a five-year period of 1999-2000 to 2003-04. Most of the municipal corporations (MCs) were generating revenue surplus and the overall resource gaps were not very large. Component-wise, tax revenue accounted for 45.2 per cent of their total own revenue, followed by non-tax revenue at 28.7 per cent. Establishment and administration expenditure accounted for about 36 per cent of total expenditure during 2000-2004. Expenditure on public works accounted for about 44 per cent of the total expenditure. Among the public works, a significant share of 19.5 per cent of the total expenditure went to roads, parks and playgrounds.

The situation is very different in the small and medium towns of India. A prime indicator of an ULB's financial health and effective autonomy is per capita own revenue receipts, which comprise tax incomes and non-tax incomes (fees, fines and user charges). The performance of ULBs in terms of this indicator in all the states covered in the PRIA study fell far below the national average of Rs. 482.10. In fact, the average figures in the states range from Rs. 123.42 to Rs. 321.60 only.

The study shows that the receipts from own sources are low and dissatisfactory in Bihar, Chhattisgarh, Haryana, Rajasthan, in both absolute and relative terms. Own source revenue was 60.5 per cent of total revenue

---

8.   RBI (2008).

receipts of municipalities. In Haryana, tax receipts formed 37.4 per cent of own revenue. Collection is poor and needs all round improvement. However, except from Narnaul, the overall collection of *tehbazari* fees and shop rent is good. Still, the income from non-tax sources is comparatively low on account of fees, fines and user charges not having been revised upwards in a long time. A similar situation is observed in Chhattisgarh where too non-tax incomes are sporadic and unpredictable and tax collection is low.

Yet, according to the RBI study, despite the apparently sound fiscal health, all the MCs spent less than what they should ideally have spent on a minimum level of civic amenities. This happened partly because of statutory obligations; the ULBs were bound to restrict their expenditure to the resources available and were also not allowed by state governments to raise debt. The average level of underspending was 76 per cent, while the extent of underspending varied between 30.78 per cent in the case of Pune and 94.43 per cent in the case of Patna. Bihar and Uttar Pradesh were the worst performers in this regard and Maharahstra and Gujarat, the best. Also, MCs such as Mumbai, Surat and Pune, which are among the best performers in terms of other financial parameters, have below average user charges. On an average, the cost recovery is below a quarter of the expenditure incurred.

Interestingly, while the MCs of large cities are earning better revenues than the small towns, the endogenous and exogenous reasons for the underspending are practically the same. Exogenous factors, over which ULBs have no control, include dependence for resources on the upper tiers of government and inadequate delegation of revenue-raising powers. Endogenous factors include inefficient revenue (tax) administration, low cost recovery and poor quality of expenditure. PRIA's study reveals that small and medium towns in India are unable to bear even their establishment cost from the revenue they collect. Revenue collected from own sources (taxes, fees, fines, charges, etc.) are no more that Rs. 200 per capita for the towns covered (the highest being Rs. 240 in Himachal Pradesh), whereas the establishment cost alone averages around Rs. 260 per capita. Other than establishment, the revenue expenditure (running expenses in other words) of municipal bodies comprise administration and operation and maintenance of civic services.

Intrinsic domestic financial strength varies widely in the five towns of Himachal Pradesh namely, Parwanoo, Bilaspur, Nagrota Bagwan, Dharamshala and Manali. In Rajasthan, property tax was abolished in January 2007, making the municipal governments more dependent on the state government for compensating them for the sudden drying up of a substantial income.

The discrepancy between the average of own source revenue in the states and the average figure for the towns studied is an indication of the difference between the financial performance of the big cities and that of the small and medium towns. This difference was found to be pretty marked in Rajasthan, which is corroborated by secondary sources. Bigger towns in the state are growing whereas the smaller ones are stagnating. It was a similar story in Chhattisgarh where big industrial cities like Durg, Bilaspur and Raipur are financially much stronger than the small towns studied. The latter are more like overgrown villages, with much of its population in very poor slums.

## Dependence on Revenue Grants

The revenue grants are mainly SFC recommended grants, establishment grants or compensation grants for withdrawn taxes. Being revenue grants they can be used for any purpose that the municipalities think fit. Usually they are used to foot establishment bills. Their surplus is very often used to finance development expenditure in the form of new infrastructure. So, the hand-outs in the form of revenue grants are effectively financing not only the day-to-day running expenses of the municipal bodies, but also much of their capital development (enhancement of infrastructure).

Most of the towns in the study show alarmingly high level of dependence on revenue grants from the state governments. The percentage of revenue grants in total revenue receipts reveals a clearer picture of dependence on revenue grants. The highest incidence of revenue grant dependence is in Rajasthan—about 90 per cent. In Haryana, the average amount of revenue grants received by the towns covered by the study was less than the state average. This implies that the grants are perhaps bigger for bigger cities. Except in Haryana, all the towns covered show a higher than 50 per cent dependence on revenue grants.

Revenue grants are given to cover the day-to-day running expenses of the ULBs, which have relatively greater freedom to spend these than capital grants that are given for a specific purpose. The type and composition of these grants have varied widely across the six states studied, yet some general commonalities do exist. The most voluminous grant in this category is the compensation for octroi, a tax that has now been abolished. This was the largest revenue earner in most cities and enough to cover establishment costs and some of the costs incurred on operation and maintenance.

In Haryana, however, some revenue grants are also given, though sporadically, to cover salary expenses. They are smaller than the octroi compensation grant, which is given as a capital grant in the state and is specifically earmarked for local development. Other grants in this category are primary education grants, other compensatory grants for entertainment tax, stamp duty, etc. There are also SFC grants that are revenue grants given by state governments at the bidding of the SFC.

A major problem with revenue grants is that they are generous and help create a culture of bailouts and dependence for the municipal bodies. They make no significant attempt to increase their own revenue collection, preferring the easy way out.

## Tax Incomes

Barring a few exceptions, the tax income of all the towns surveyed by this study is alarmingly low. The maximum per capita tax that the ULBs recover is only about Rs. 160 in Himachal Pradesh. It is the lowest in Rajasthan, only Rs. 11. The argument that small towns are more likely to have a low tax base does not apply here, because equally small towns in certain other states of India perform far better. For instance, Phaltan municipality of Maharashtra, whose population is only 55,000, collects Rs. 394 per capita with an insignificant economic base. Thus, while demographics and economic base matter, it seems administrative will prevails over these other factors. In many cases, elected officers of the municipality are usually reluctant to impose and raise additional taxes and strengthen the tax net, to retain their popularity.

**Figure 4.2**

*Tax Income in the Small Towns Studied*

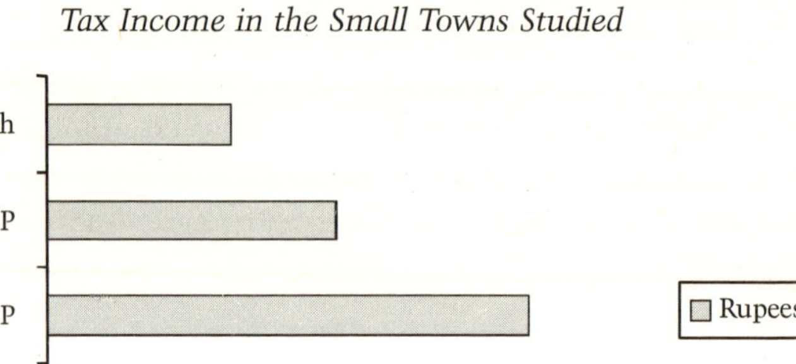


Property tax collection is remarkably high in Parwanoo, average in Dharamshala but miserably low in Bilaspur and Nagrota Bagwan. Tax collection in Himachal Pradesh looks better because of the very efficient and exemplary tax imposition and collection by the Parwanoo Municipal Council. There, the tax evaluation method is objective, transparent and non-discretionary. Citizens are remarkably aware and enthusiastic about tax payment, even availing of discounts for early payment.

There is all round substantial dependence on revenue and capital grants for recurrent and developmental expenditure. This dependence is decreasing in some towns such as Parwanoo but increasing in some others such as Dharamshala. In almost all the municipal bodies studied, octroi compensation grant has been stopped as soon as the municipality has started receiving state finance commission grants.

Himachal also shows a large revenue-expenditure gap, which has been rising steadily. This has serious implications for the financial viability and sustainability of its municipalities. Own revenue receipts covered only 35.12 per cent of municipal expenditure, which is much lower than the average for sample states (83.6 per cent). Per capita revenue deficit of Rs. 147.32 was the highest in the country and rose by 14.7 per cent from

1997-98 to 2001-02. This is an alarming situation and needs to be corrected on a priority basis.

Haryana is also a better performer, not so much because of property tax, but because of the significant share of its own stamp duty that is allotted to them. Except in Narnaul, there is impressive collection of *tehbazari* fees and shop rent. Still, per capita revenue receipts for municipalities in 2001-02 was Rs. 343.27, of which per capita own revenue was Rs. 207.8—less than half of the 23 states covered in the Mathur and Thakur study or Rs. 482.10—and has also risen at the slowest. Own source revenue (OSR) as a percentage of total revenue receipts of municipalities was 60.5 per cent. Tax receipts formed 37.4 per cent of own revenue receipts, the per capita figure being only Rs. 76.7, which is extremely low and dissatisfactory. The PRIA study found revenue grants very small and barely enough to cover running expenses although received as establishment/salary grants. Octroi compensation is given but in the form of a capital grant specifically earmarked for development.

The per capita state transfer to ULBs in Haryana was Rs. 135.5 in 2001-02. Transfers formed 40 per cent of municipal revenues in Haryana, which is moderate as compared to states like Rajasthan. More alarming is that the growth rate of transfers is extremely high, 18.6 per cent during 1997-98 to 2001-02.

Rajasthan performs very poorly. Tax devolution as per cent of state own tax revenue is only 1.97 per cent. Per capita own revenue declined from Rs. 150.27 in 1998-99 to Rs. 123.42 in 2002-03. Local revenue from property tax especially holds immense potential in Rajasthan and needs to be realised in earnest. The existing rates of house tax and non-tax levies are very low and unrealistic and need to be totally revamped to make them reflect the cost of service provision incurred by the municipalities.

Rajasthan is a typical example of a state with high per capita transfers but low per capita municipal revenue. In spite of being a low revenue state, the government transfers much larger funds on per capita basis to ULBs. A cursory look at the state of municipal finance in Rajasthan shows that the dependence of municipal bodies on state transfers is extremely high; the share was as high as 83.3 per cent of local budgets on an average during the period of study.

In Andhra Pradesh, the share of tax revenues was nearly 30 per cent in 1995-96 but declined to 20 per cent in 2000-01, while the share of non-tax and assigned revenues together has gone up from about 27 per cent to 31 per cent. The share of plan grants has fluctuated wildly every year, ranging from 15 per cent to 30 per cent. The income from own sources of the municipalities has gone down to 51 per cent in 2000-01. Most worryingly, the share of property tax revenue declined from 52 per cent of own revenue to reach 39 per cent in 2000-01.

## Non-Tax Incomes

As per the PRIA study, it is difficult to spot a definite trend in non-tax incomes which comprise fees, user charges and fines. In most municipalities, such incomes may be high but are also sporadic and volatile. In this respect, Himachal Pradesh's relatively better performance is mainly on account of shop rent, bank interest and regular collection of map approval fees and miscellaneous fees for other charges.

**Figure 4.3**

*Non-Tax Revenues in Small Towns (PRIA Study)*

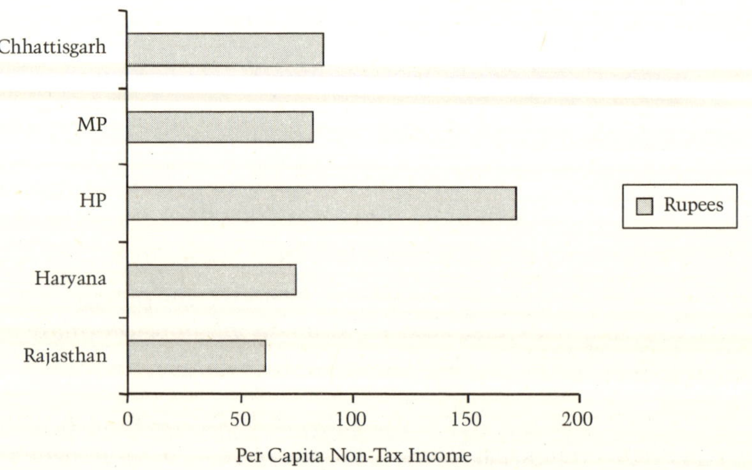


Per Capita Non-Tax Income

Within the municipal own taxes, property tax is more buoyant and high yielding source of tax revenue in the non-octroi states of India. On the other hand, it is not buoyant and inelastic in states where octroi rules and is the main source of municipal income. A study on property tax conducted by NIUA (2004) reveals that the receipt from property tax is low on account of legal and administrative problems, which plague the property tax system. Various studies on this subject show that in aggregate terms, about 40-60 per cent of the potential of this tax is realised and it continues to be plagued by problems of assessment, valuation exemption policies and limits imposed on rents of properties under the Rent Control Acts, disputes etc. On the other hand, the income from non-tax sources are volatile and sporadic, therefore very unreliable as a steady source of income. The collection is not at its best because of shortage of staff and political will. The share of non-tax revenues has increased despite the decrease in share of domestic resources. Although municipalities have placed a greater emphasis on user charges and other sources of revenues in recent years, user charges for services are not levied in any systematic way and the cost of service delivery is not met.[9]

## Octroi

Octroi levies have been a major determinant of municipal revenue incomes in several states, especially in the north-western states of Gujarat, Maharashtra and Punjab. Abolition of octroi early this decade without any substitute has shrunk the revenue base of municipalities in Haryana, Odisha, Rajasthan and altered the revenue profile of municipalities in Gujarat and Maharashtra. The latter not only had high incomes accruing from octroi, but also incurred heavy expenditure; they are responsible for water supply and sewerage system and run hospitals, transport and some other high-utility services. The states that abolished octroi have not been able to find an alternative for their ULBs as buoyant as octroi. Several have experimented, such as Karnataka going in for entry tax and Tamil Nadu levying a surcharge on sales tax for the Chennai Municipal Corporation. But states such as Uttar Pradesh and Andhra Pradesh have not attempted instituting any major tax in the place of octroi. Even the compensations for abolition have been abysmally low.

---

9.  Ray (2006).

**Table 4.5**

*Octroi in the Finances of Municipalities, 2001-02*

| State | Octroi Compensation (Rs. lakh) | Impact of Octroi on Municipal Own Revenue Base (%) |
|---|---|---|
| Haryana | 6479.6 | 53.5 |
| Odisha | 9482.6 | 93.2 |
| Rajasthan | 37036.1 | 358.2 |

*Source:* Mathur and Thakur (2004).

## Global Tax-Sharing

One major recommendation in this respect is "global tax-sharing". In order to overcome the problems of the earlier system of devolution and strengthen the financial condition of local bodies, the finance commissions of nine states, including Assam, Karnataka, Madhya Pradesh, Rajasthan, Tamil Nadu and Uttar Pradesh, have come forward with the principle of global sharing of state tax revenue. The report of the first SFC of Uttar Pradesh highlights that "the earlier practice of sharing revenues from specific taxes, tolls, fees, etc., affected adversely the finances of local bodies." The important dimension in the concept of global sharing of revenues in the total tax/non-tax receipts of the state government is that a fixed proportion (specific share) of state income generated from its own revenues (i.e., total divisible pool) is shared with the local bodies.

---

*The Concept of Global Sharing*

The system of global sharing has distinct advantages. It allows state governments to tax the more buoyant and elastic tax sources and guarantees a regular, rising and predicable flow of revenues to local bodies...Under global sharing, local bodies automatically share the buoyancy in state's tax revenues. This system also has the advantages of transparency, objectively, predictable and regularity. It is also helpful in annual budgetary exercises both at the state and the local body levels.

*Source:* NIUA (2005).

---

Transfer through global sharing is preferred to transfer through assignment of certain taxes because of two reasons. First, the state government may not make efforts for restructuring the assigned taxes for raising more funds, since either full or a large part of revenue from such taxes would go to local bodies. This has happened in the case of land revenue, which is mostly passed on to rural local bodies. Second, global tax-sharing is preferred as local bodies then get a share in the tax buoyancy of the state government, be it for structural and efficiency improvement or for improvement in business climate and per capita income.

The concept of global sharing involves the creation of a divisible pool at the state level. But the definition of the divisible pool varies from state to state, thanks to varied interpretations by the SFCs. Ideally, this should include the net proceeds of all taxes, fees, tolls, etc., levied by the respective state governments.

**Table 4.6**

*Tax-Sharing Recommended by SFCs*

**1st SFC**
- 5 states recommended for global sharing of tax and non-tax revenue;
- 6 states went for only tax revenue sharing.

**2nd SFC**
- 6 states recommended for both tax and non-tax sharing;
- 8 states opted for sharing of tax revenue only.

**3rd SFC**
- 2 states recommended for tax and non-tax revenue sharing;
- 3 states went for sharing of tax revenue only.

  Constitution provides for distribution of taxes, duties, tolls and fees.

## Little Difference in Finances in Two Decades

We see how over the past two decades, and despite the 74th CAA, municipal bodies have had few sources other than their own to depend upon for meeting fund needs. In 1986-87, on an average, the municipal bodies spent[10] Rs. 143.14 per capita on operation and maintenance (O&M) of various services, much lower than the norms laid down by the Zakaria Committee or Rs. 204.74 for cities with population of 1-5 lakh and Rs. 239.25 for higher population. The spending level was particularly low in water supply and sanitation, only Rs. 47.50 per head against the norm of Rs. 126.27, just a measly 37 per cent of the norm.

---

10.  NIUA (1989).

The Sixth Finance Commission first considered upgrade of standards through a grant-in-aid. The Eighth FC recommended nine sectors for upgrade—police, education, jails, tribal administration, health, judicial administration, district & revenue administration, training & treasury, and accounts administration. It did not recommend any grant-in-aid. The Ninth CFC made a significant departure—recommended one time grants for Maharashtra and West Bengal for slum redevelopment, and higher levels of grants-in-aid for education and health sectors. So the Ninth CFC recognised the problems of slums, environment, revenues of municipal bodies and the disappointing levels of social services in the report and that these issues should be dealt with not only through plan subventions but in a broader framework involving both the Planning Commission as well as the Finance Commission.

Mathur and Thakur (2004) point out that absence of autonomy or low discretion coefficient in matters relating to tax rate setting is one of the highlights and key shortcoming of the functioning of municipal governments. "While the municipal revenue base in India may fulfill the criteria for the determination of a local tax base, that is, the principles of residence and benefit taxation, low mobility, and stability over the period of business cycle, and while it may even create a link between service use and tax payment, it is controlled and regulated by state governments. Most state governments lay down local tax policies, ranging from choice of tax rates, capping them and determining who to include or exclude from those taxes."

## Quite Absolute State Control

While the Constitutional framework and general administrative-political reform reluctance does hamper effective decentralisation in India, there are several other reasons why the state continues to morally dominate over local bodies. We sum up the reasons:

- High dependence of urban local bodies on government grants/funds due to their weak finances.

- Urban services are considered as basic or essential (public/social goods, natural monopolies) for a good quality of life for citizens. Higher governments cannot risk that due to inefficiencies and inabilities of local bodies.

- Also, urban sector has higher productivity and contribution to overall economic growth and hence, the state needs to have control over its development.

- Provision through markct operations is bound to leave out a large number of urban population who are disadvantaged and lack access and can lead to political unrest.

- Political non-exclusivity.

- Long-term capital-intensive investment needed in urban infrastructure to ensure good quality of life in urban area which only the state can provide.

- Long gestation and payback periods associated with urban infrastructure project necessitate state intervention.

- Externality induced pricing.

- Inelastic demand for urban service as they are basic human necessities.

Also, India is perhaps the only established democracy where the local governments do not function as a separate political executive system. Barring some states, such as West Bengal, Madhya Pradesh and Chhattisgarh which have created a cabinet type municipal political executive system (mayor-in-council), though with no substantial powers, other states are still continuing with an appointed executive functionary who is a bureaucrat accountable to the state government and not to local government or to local people.

# 5 Neglecting Development

*Spending Woes of Municipal Bodies*

In the greater part of this decade, due to fiscal stress brought about by the Fifth Pay Commission awards, rising interest liabilities and subsidies, states have been forced to meet their revenue expenditure by cutting back development as well as plan expenditure. While the fiscal reform facility introduced by the finance commissions and the introduction of VAT have had a salubrious effect on the revenue accounts of the states, bringing about surpluses in several of them in the past two years, the problem can resurface again during economic downturns. Some of the constituents of revenue expenditure are inflexible and therefore tough to reduce. Also, development expenditures have been neglected for too long and must be taken up in earnest.

The performance of municipalities in terms of expenditure is not much different from their revenue-earning skills. Even though over 90 per cent of municipal expenditure is met from own sources of revenues, expenditures have been shooting up of late. In non-octroi states, the ratio of domestic revenue to total expenditure has been declining. The situation is aggravated by the limited fiscal powers of the ULBs.

As for municipal expenditures, according to the TFC report, as a proportion of the combined gross state domestic product (GSDP), they have risen gradually from 0.74 per cent in 1997-98 to 0.75 per cent in 2001-02. Even at 0.75 per cent of the GSDP, municipal expenditure levels are extremely low. Of the larger states, Maharashtra, Punjab, Gujarat and Goa have higher per capita municipal expenditures and a higher expenditure to GSDP ratio. Coming next at the median are Andhra Pradesh, Kerala, West Bengal and Tamil Nadu.

In a 2006 paper, Oommen (2006) analyses the trends in fiscal decentralisation in India focusing on the 15 non-special category states based on data from the TFC report. He finds that the total expenditure of local government as a proportion of the combined expenditure of Union, state and local governments declined from 6.4 per cent in 1998-99 to 5.1 per cent in 2002-03. This, he argues, compares poorly with advanced countries, where local governments normally account for about 20-35 per cent of total government expenditure.

### Table 5.1

*Broad Heads of Expenses and their Share for 35 Municipal Corporations Over 1999-2004*

| Expenditure Category | Expenditure Items |
| --- | --- |
| Establishment expenditure | Staff salaries. Allowances, wages, pension and retirement benefits etc. |
| Administrative expenditure | Rents, rates and taxes. Office maintenance, communications, books and periodicals, printing & stationary. Travel expenditure. Law charges etc. |
| Operations & maintenance | Power & fuel, bulk purchases, stores, hire charges, repairs & expenditure maintenance and interest payments made on loans. |
| Capital expenditure | Buildings, water supply & sewerage, energy/lighting. Solid waste management, roads, bridges, culverts, causeways, health & sanitation, parks and recreation spaces. Furniture & fittings, tools & plant, equipment etc., principal repayments of loans. |
| Other expenditure | Miscellaneous expenses not accounted for in the above. |

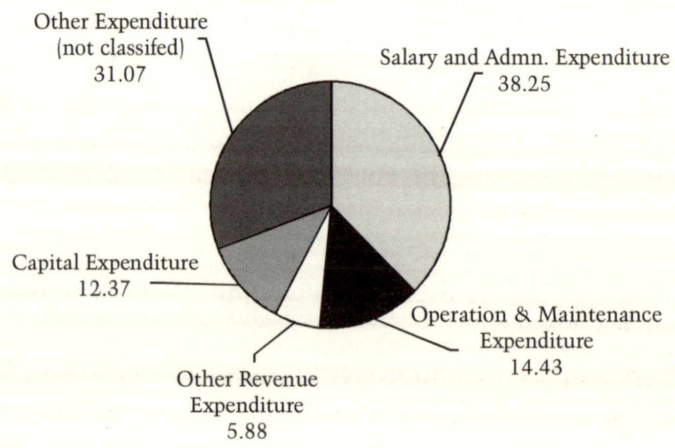


*Source:*  RBI (2008). *Budgets of MCs.*

## Uncontrolled Establishment Costs

Table 5.1 shows the usual heads of expenditure and their share in 35 municipal corporations from the 2008 RBI study. The trends here echo national findings. The most significant attribute of municipal expenditure, in which they echo their state counterparts, is that on an average, expenditure on establishment—mainly salaries and wages—is responsible for 54.2 per cent of the total (38.25 per cent in the case of the 35 MCs in Table 5.1.) Within that, it can be as high as 80.4 per cent in Madhya Pradesh, 69.7 per cent in Haryana and 65 per cent in Uttar Pradesh.

At over half of the total revenue expenditure, establishment expenditure eats away the bulk of the finances available to municipalities for meeting its running expenses. The major component of establishment is the salary bill, which leaves little funds to operate and maintain basic services. Since salary bills are steady and recurrent expenditure, municipalities can do little else but keep its growth in check by freezing employment.

**Box 5.1**

*No Work, All Pay at MCD: Ghost Employees Lose
Civic Body Rs. 17 Crore a Month*

In November 2009, it was revealed that a huge chunk of ghost employees, who didn't punch in their attendance but had been regularly paid salaries, was costing the Municipal Corporation of Delhi (MCD) Rs. 17 crore every month. The MCD has now decided to make all payments online as well as extend its current biometric attendance system to all employees, including Education department employees and daily wage workers, by introducing mobile devices.

In fact, a series of RTI queries made by social activist and advocate Vivek Kumar Garg revealed that MCD actually tops the corruption chart with about 4,300 cases and is followed by Delhi government, Delhi Development Authority and Delhi Police. The MCD's vigilance department said as many as 4,299 cases were pending against 3,350 officials, of which 1,435 cases were by anti-corruption branch of the Delhi government, Police and CBI whereas 2,877 such cases were registered by its own vigilance wing.

*Source:* *http://www.indianexpress.com/news/mcd-tops-in-corruption-cases-followed-by-delhi-govt-and-dda/526666/*

*http://www.indianexpress.com/news/to-log-out-corruption-mcd-to-put-in-place-new-online-payment-system/553812/0*

However, not all establishment expenditures are unproductive. Some kinds of establishment expenditure, such as salaries of health personnel, school teachers and sweepers, add to the services of health, education and sanitation offered by municipal bodies. Annual growth in this is essential and cannot be discouraged. However, an excess of clerical and bureaucratic staff plague municipal bodies across India. Appointments are made less on the basis of norms and vacancies but by ad hoc decisions based on nepotism, creating an unnecessary burden on the municipal exchequer. This ails bigger municipal corporations more, as the experience of Municipal Corporation of Delhi proves (see Box 5.1), but small town functionaries too are afflicted by this malaise though to a lesser extent.

Establishment expenditures are as high as 80.4 per cent in Madhya Pradesh, 69.7 per cent in Haryana, 50.6 per cent in Odisha and 65 per cent in Uttar Pradesh. In many states, even own resource revenue fails to cover establishment expenditure and they depend on state governments for meeting the cost of establishment.

This obviously leaves very little resources for operations and maintenance of urban infrastructure facilities, which is the second important component of revenue expenditure, accounting for 39.93 per cent of the total municipal expenditure.

In such a situation, it is easy to predict that capital expenditures would be low. In fact, even for the 35 MCs, it comes to, on an average, only 12.37 per cent of the total expenditure during 1999-2004.

On an average, municipal underspending (measured by the Zakaria Committee norms) is 130 per cent, which largely explains why urban services in India, be it water and sanitation or road conditions, are so poor and inadequate compared to most cities in the world. Mathur *et al.*, 2000 estimate that even if we do not measure against the Zakaria Committee norms, "average per capita expenditures (daily) ranging between 20 paise and Rs. 2.25 can not, by any standard, be expected to deliver services that would satisfy the needs of either the urban households or other non-domestic consumers". Figure 5.1 shows how even the 35 MCs with relatively good fiscal balance, neglected the expenditure on essential municipal functions such as provision of water supply, drainage, sewerage, health & sanitation and solid waste management in preference to spending on discretionary items such as education and parks.

**Figure 5.1**

*Expenditure on Public Works and their Share for*
*35 Municipal Corporations Over 1999-2004*

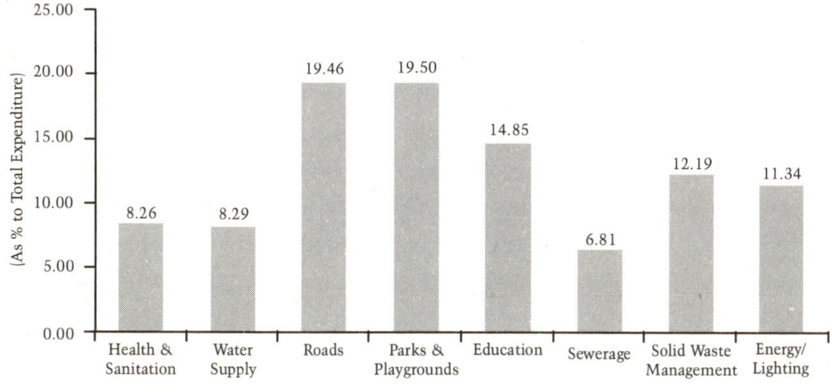


*Source:* RBI (2008). *Budgets of MCs.*

## Capital Account

Capital account in municipal finance deals with financial flows related to investment in physical or social infrastructure building in the town.

Capital inflows to a municipality occur either from its own sources (mostly by sale of its assets), by incurring new loans, or from capital grants given by Central or state governments for specific purpose (usually creation of assets in the nature of physical infrastructure). Most of these towns are too small and poor to qualify for receiving substantial loans from other financial institutions. They also do not earn much by selling their limited assets. So, barring exceptions, the main capital inflow usually comes from capital grants given by state or from centrally sponsored schemes, e.g., Integrated Development of Small and Medium Towns (IDSMT), National Slum Development Programme (NSDP), etc.

Capital expenditure occurs when expenditure is incurred to acquire new assets (usually physical infrastructure assets, but often human assets like training of personnel, or employment generation schemes for poor), extend existing infrastructure (such as purchasing new streetlight posts, new sewer, lines etc.). Capital expenditure is of utmost importance for the improvement of the city and provision of basic services for the growing population. Each municipality must do its utmost to undertake new development works at all times. The resources for this may come from its own capital income from aforementioned sources, or it may be financed by surplus from the revenue account (called operating surplus).

For the majority of the towns surveyed across the states, the capital account shows deficit, which is coexistent with a revenue surplus. So part of the developmental needs of the city are being financed by the revenue surplus. However, unfortunately, that surplus rests almost solely on the revenue grants received from the state government (mainly for octroi compensation). A few municipalities especially in Chhattisgarh and Haryana tend to have surplus on the capital account. This shows that developmental expenditures are not being undertaken even though funds are available. There are likely to be bottlenecks in municipal bodies' attempts to undertake expenditure. They should be looked into. This is because the apparent surplus may be owing to accounting lapses.

Account keeping of capital expenditures is frequently not done properly, being under the jurisdiction of the respective engineering departments. This also warrants attention. A few towns in Madhya Pradesh and Chhattisgarh unfortunately have a deficit on both capital and revenue accounts. These deficits are usually met by temporary borrowing from extraordinary account, or from revenue grants in the following year.

## Extraordinary Account

The extraordinary account is maintained by ULBs to document liability related parallel financial flows, over which the municipal body itself has no direct claim.

Receipts in the extraordinary account represent financial inflows that are not a part of the municipality's own income. These consist of, for example, inflows into various security deposits that have to be refunded one day, revenues collected on behalf of other agencies (e.g. education cess on behalf of the state government), recovery of advances, or salary deductions that are returnable.

Outflows from this account, for example, refund of deposits, giving of advances which it will get back, payment into its various funds (e.g. sinking fund) etc., do not constitute the municipal body's expenditure. Ideally the extraordinary account should be revenue neutral. However, for most of the municipalities, this is in deficit, implying that the actual expenditures are more than what is apparent. In some cases, these are in surplus, which means that the revenues with the municipality are less than they seem. To prevent this development, advances given should be promptly recovered, and deposits (and other liabilities) should be promptly refunded.

In many municipalities, particularly in Himachal Pradesh and Madhya Pradesh, an analysis of extraordinary accounts was not possible due to lack of reliable financial records in the municipal budgets.

## Functional Analysis

Except in Himachal Pradesh, and in few towns in the other states (e.g. Karauli in Rajasthan), figures were available in adequate detail to permit an analysis of the financial flows in each budget head (corresponding to each function) of the municipality. This is expected to reveal the municipality's priority, as far as expenditure on basic service provision is concerned. Almost without exception, the lion's share of the municipal body's funds was spent on public works (at least 75 per cent), consisting of roads, bridges, drainage, sewerage, water supply, sanitation, streetlights and public buildings. A lot of expenditure is usually incurred in this department for payment of electricity bill for streetlights and construction of roads. Some significant expenditure is also usually diverted to the health department, which spends principally on salaries. Other departments/functions such as solid waste management, urban environment and forestry (comprising parks and gardens, pollution control, etc.), civic amenities etc., suffer gross neglect, causing cities to remain dirty and polluted, helping to breed disease. To remedy this neglect and ensure balanced development of the city, the SFCs could recommend some specific-purpose capital grants and make sure that crucial works such as solid waste management and other civic amenities are taken up.

## Accounting Systems and Budget Documents

The system of financial reporting, record keeping, accounting and budget document preparation is in a deplorable condition in most municipalities. In all municipalities covered in the present study, accounts are kept using the single entry cash based system. Almost without exception, accounts were found to be handwritten. Rajasthan was found to have very poor accounting practices, with accounts not only being handwritten but there was also no computer or typewriter support in some municipal boards.

Accounting formats and budgeting classification of all items of revenue and expenditure were devoid of logic. Items were clubbed together in composite totals without mentioning the break-up of constituents. Most of the inconvenience was caused because of lack of uniformity in budget document preparation and classification of financial flows among the states. Too many variations made comparative financial analysis very difficult.

It was unequivocally clear that poor accounting systems made transparency and accountability very difficult. Countrywide accounting reforms should be initiated to bring about data entry in standardised, simple and logical formats. For this, training of municipal accountants may be recommended.

In each state, problems were different. In Rajasthan, the language used and terms used in the budgets was unnecessarily cumbersome and complex, making any analysis difficult. In Himachal Pradesh, some aggregated heads, whose components were not expressed, did not permit any meaningful functional analysis. It is recommended that each item of revenue and expenditure be recorded separately.

By contrast, there is a problem of plenty in the budget documents in Madhya Pradesh, with far too much detail expressed under multitude of different heads, entered in a disorderly mess that make analysis very difficult. They must forthwith switch to some broad and logical grouping. In Haryana, capital expenditures, particularly those from capital grants, are not recorded properly and are compiled and maintained by the engineering department. In Chhattisgarh, the data recorded in the budget documents are quite devoid of credibility and therefore, the analysis is bound to be sub-optimal.

But the worst scenario of financial record keeping and accounting was encountered in Bihar, where a budgeting process is yet to begin in the towns surveyed. Financial records have not been compiled in most of them due to lack of adequate staff. Sporadic and unreliable figures of receipts and payments have been scribbled into ledger books that are not often available, let alone being accessible to the public, and even lost. This did not permit any credible financial analysis of the municipalities surveyed. Thus, it was abundantly clear to the researchers that the lack of a clear and transparent accounting system contributed a great deal to the rampant corruption in urban governance in India.

## Corruption

Scarce resources of the ULBs are, to an unfortunately large extent, frittered away by corruption. Its presence throttles urban governance and city development, though its magnitude, nature and character vary widely from state to state. Drawing attention to the large-scale corruption in local bodies in the state, the first SFC of Goa said that people did not favour transferring more powers and authority in the hands of *sarpanches* and elected representatives who were misappropriating funds and abusing their powers. The Commission recommended appointing a retired High Court judge as an ombudsman to promote autonomy of local bodies as well as rights of citizens.[1]

Even the PRIA study found corruption rampant in the towns surveyed. The corruption in Bihar municipal bodies is usually carried out by an intricate nexus of unholy alliances between state government officers around the nucleus of district administration and local government officers (elected and executive). So strong and well-knit is the dragnet that any sporadic attempt by an honest officer to stall corruption is easily scuttled.

In Himachal Pradesh, development works and expenditure on regular provision of civic services are concentrated around the residences of municipal officers, to the neglect of the rest of the city. In Haryana, some interviews have reported nexus between municipal officials, contractors and private operators to deliver basic services (usually sanitation and solid waste management). In addition, capital expenditure records are poorly maintained and are kept solely with the engineering department. They are extremely difficult to access. The fact that there is no summary of grant flows available indicates the lack of interest in tracking grant flows. The

---

1. Mishra *op. cit.*

stubborn resistance of the officers in sharing financial records relating to expenditure from capital grants is worthy of special mention.

## Bridging the Resource Gap

An NIUA review,[2] sponsored by UN Inter Agency Working Group on Decentralisation (UNIAWG-D), of decentralisation measures that seek to empower ULBs in 28 urban areas, comprising 25 towns in Tamil Nadu, Mumbai, Pune and Ahmedabad where decentralisation had been understood to have helped improve governance and led to greater transparency in functioning, drew several interesting conclusions that we discuss below.

First, given the openness of the economy of the cities, it is impossible for the ULBs to prepare a development plan without a regional perspective, proposed at a higher level such as region or district. Although most states have constituted the district planning committees (DPCs), they do not have as yet a functioning standard. The situation is worse as far as the metropolitan planning committees (MPCs) are concerned. As a result, the ULBs have been forced to take decisions in an institutional vacuum. That has not led to desired results as local bodies neither have the technical competence nor the information base to take decisions with regard to location of industrial unit, its technology and production links.

Second, the ULBs also do not have the capability to assess the long-term cost implications of any possible contracts they might enter into with private companies for the people or the local economy. Nor has the state government been cooperative in this regard by providing technical assistance to ULBs for assessing, say, the long-term implications of land deals or appropriate environmental safeguards.

Special purpose parastatal agencies, through which substantial developmental funds are routed, have turned out to be an important hurdle in decentralisation, hampering innovative urban management practices. But the ULBs are unlikely to interfere. A similar hurdle comes in the form of standing committees (SC), which are responsible for day-to-day decision-making. Neither the state governments nor the state finance commissions

---

2.   NIUA (1997).

**Figure 5.2**

*Financing Urban Infrastructure*

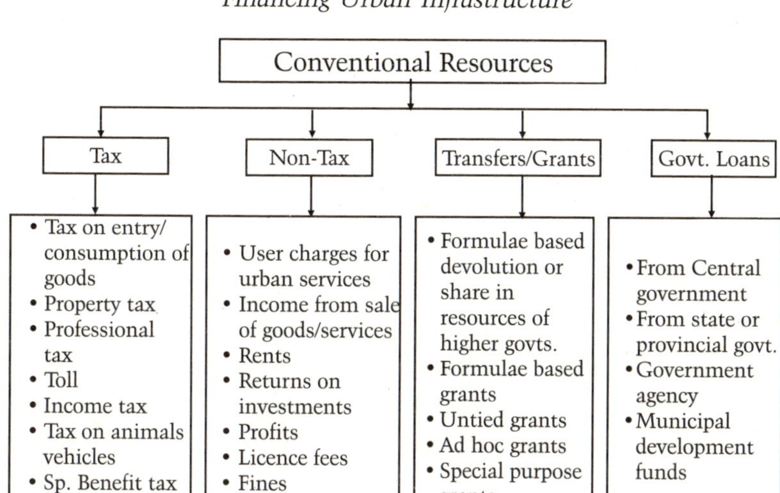


(SFCs) have paid attention to the fact that the 74th CAA or the supporting legislations at the state level do not lay down how many or how long such committees might function to optimise their inputs.

But the most significant criticism of the decentralisation model is that financial resources are being devolved without keeping a holistic view of urban development and without examining how the functions will be assigned to and carried out by local bodies and what will be their implications. The new policy of the local bodies or ward committees (within the cities) providing basic amenities, as per the paying capacity of the residents, has contributed to lower norms and standards of the services and put public health at risk.

Also, withdrawal of government support and relegation of provision of the services to the market or sub-contracting arrangements with private companies have led to clear inequalities across regions and classes of settlements. In fact, inter-state disparity has become starker. The ULBs, especially in the backward states, are not financially equipped to invest in strengthening their planning system. Most of the ULBs have fallen back on financial intermediaries and credit rating agencies, which have created more trouble by imposing stringent conditions regarding project priorities and disbursal of own budgetary resources.

Only a few large cities with good economic basc have been able to mobilise additional resources owing to the CAA by raising new taxes or tax rates and tapping the capital market by floating structured debt obligations (SDOs) or through borrowings from international organisations. But the small and medium towns, which have a much higher percentage of households not having access to basic amenities and therefore must forthwith provide them, are the ones which have been left out in the cold in the new dispensation.

The community-based projects like Slum Networking Project in Ahmedabad (SNP) have earned unprecedented acclaim nationally and a few of these are cited as examples of best practices at international level. Unfortunately, these have been taken up only in a few cities, and even there, restricted to a few localities. Their replicability at the national level has remained questionable, due to absence of organisational structure for community mobilisation and lack of commitment of supportive funds.

---

**Box 5.2**

*A Street-Cleaning Vehicle for the One Road in Janjgir!*

There's little to distinguish Janjgir town (in Chhattisgarh) from a village, except for one 30 ft long main road from the station and the fact that it is the district headquarters. It doesn't even have a movie theatre. A quarter of its people live in slums. The President of the Janjgir Municipal Council, Motilal Dahariya, who is directly elected, says, "We have no sources for revenue in Janjgir. There is no factory from which we can collect tax. We do have property tax and mandi tax. The water tax is fixed at Rs. 50 per month, because there are no water meters. We get octroi compensation from the state government." During his tenure, he managed to install a water filtration plant but the MC had to take a loan. As most of the local funds go towards the interest from that loan, the *nagarpalika* runs out of money to pay salaries in the last month of the financial year. On the other hand, the council seemed to have enough money to buy a special street-cleaning vehicle which is used on the lone *pucca* road!

*Source:* Sharma (2009).

# 6 | Developing as Growth Engines

*Urban Reform and the Role
of Municipal Bodies*

It is well-known that India's cities are such dynamic growth engines that if the local governments set their houses in order, they will be able to acquire sufficient resources for their own redevelopment on commercial terms. India's urban system is the second largest in the global hierarchy and is said to have a potential of producing 70 per cent of the country's gross domestic product by the year 2020.[1]

Despite a significant contribution of cities and towns to the GDP and national and regional growth and productivity, they remain grossly deficient in basic services. According to the 58th Round of the National Sample Survey carried out during July–December 2002, more than 92 per cent of urban households used electricity, even if many of these connections could well be illegal. Yet, 34 per cent of urban households did not have tap water within the premises; 18 per cent of households did not have access to a toilet, and only 59 per cent of households used garbage collection facility provided by local authorities. The garbage collection efficiency is low and only 7 per cent of solid waste is put to some kind of treatment.

This situation is aggravated by the migration pressure on towns, cities and metros alike, leading to what is called the "urbanisation of rural poverty". In many states such as Maharashtra, Karnataka, Kerala and so on, as Planning Commission figures based on the 2004-05 National Sample Survey suggest, urban poverty is far higher than rural. In Andhra Pradesh and Rajasthan, in fact, the number of people living below the poverty line is twice that in rural areas. Urban poverty alleviation and slum development are regarded as legitimate functions of urban local bodies according to the 74th Amendment Act, yet few municipal bodies have either resources or reason to devote them to this function.

---

1. Mathur and Thakur (2004).

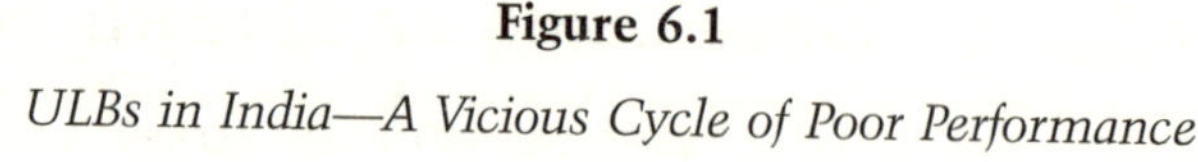

**Figure 6.1**

*ULBs in India—A Vicious Cycle of Poor Performance*

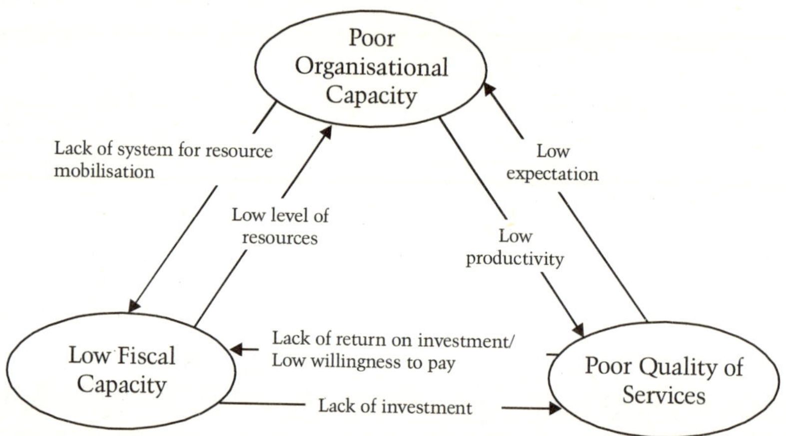


The idea behind urban reforms is to encourage construction of housing, make land easily available for all purposes, to improve municipal finances for developing civic services and urban infrastructure and finally to enable urban local bodies, particularly municipal corporations, to raise resources from the market. The urban reform process was initiated during the Tenth Plan (2001-2006) via memorandums of understanding between the Centre and the state governments that spelt out areas in which urban reforms had to be undertaken in municipal finances and administration. The Centre created the Urban Reforms Incentive Fund, with an outlay of Rs. 500 crore for 2002-03. The release of funds in tranches was tied to the total package of reforms in the MoUs and not just the individual items. The goals set for the end of Tenth Plan were:

- Repeal of Urban Land Ceiling and Regulation Act at the state level.

- Rationalisation of stamp duty in phases to bring down to not more than 5 per cent.

- Reforms of rent control laws to stimulate private investment in urban residential housing.

- Introduction of computerised process of registration of documents.

- Reform in property tax to make it the biggest source of revenue and its effective implementation to ensure collections reached at least 85 per cent of tax demand.

- Levy of user charges so as to cover the full cost of O&M.

- Introduction of double entry system of accounting in urban local bodies.

However, the scheme failed to take off and the fund did not become fully operational. This was followed by the current JNNURM, which remains equally hampered. It is important that the Central government bring out a status paper on the patchy implementation of urban reforms so far, highlighting the progress, constraints on these reforms and the measures necessary for accelerating the reform process.

## JNNURM still a Non-Starter

That the task of urban reform in India, so crucially tied with municipal performance, is gargantuan and extremely difficult is brought out significantly by the current status of the JNNURM, the ambitious seven-year central scheme to upgrade urban infrastructure launched in December 2005. While grants from the Union government are to constitute 35-80 per cent of the financing plan, the Mission targets an investment in urban infrastructure and basic services of over Rs. 1 lakh crore.

Reforms in urban governance are central to the implementation of JNNURM. Projects can pertain to urban renewal, water supply and sanitation, sewerage and solid waste management, urban transport, development of heritage areas, preservation of water bodies, and housing and basic amenities to the poor. The key reform to be pursued at the state level is implementing the decentralisation measures envisaged in the 1992 amendment. Under JNNURM, following are the key reform goals at the ULB level to be achieved after seven years, which largely echo those of the Tenth Plan urban reforms incentive scheme:

- Adoption of modern, accrual-based double entry system of accounting in ULBs.

- Introduction of system of e-governance using IT applications like GIS (Geospatial Information System) and MIS (Management Information System) for core services provided by ULBs/parastatals, resulting in cheaper and faster delivery processes.

- City-wide framework for planning and governance will be established and become operational. Financially self-sustaining agencies for urban governance and service delivery will be established, through reforms to major revenue instruments.

- Reform of property tax with GIS, so that it becomes major source of revenue for ULBs and arrangements for its effective implementation so that collection efficiency reaches at least 85 per cent within the Mission period.

- Levy of reasonable user charges by ULBs/parastatals with the objective that full cost of operation and maintenance is collected within the Mission period. However, cities/towns in the northeast and other special category states may recover at least 50 per cent of operation and maintenance charges initially. These cities/towns should graduate to full O&M cost recovery in a phased manner.

- Internal earmarking within local body budgets for basic services to the urban poor.

- Provision of basic services to urban poor including security of tenure at affordable prices, improved housing, water supply, sanitation and ensuring delivery of other already existing universal services of the government for education, health and social security.

Under JNNURM, says the Economic Survey 2008-09,[2] a Memorandum of Agreement (MoA) for urban reform agenda has been signed with 62 mission cities and six ULBs falling under the urban agglomerations and which have undertaken reforms contributing to sustainable functioning of local bodies. These reforms include comprehensive land titling legislation in Rajasthan, creation of a municipal cadre-municipal accounts service in Andhra Pradesh, setting up of urban transport fund in Surat and Pimpri-Chinchwad and setting up of urban transport authority in Hyderabad, Jaipur, Chennai, Bangalore and Mumbai. ULBs have initiated various steps to improve collection of property tax and user charges. Mission cities in

---

2. GoI (2009).

states such as West Bengal, Maharashtra, Kerala and Gujarat have adopted public-private partnership (PPP) through appropriate policies and projects as a part of the reform agenda. PPP initiatives have been taken by Indore, Vadodara, Pune and Ahmedabad for establishing city bus services and in Kochi in solid waste management.

**Table 6.1**

*JNNURM at a Glance*

| | |
|---|---|
| Number of cities covered under JNNURM | 65 |
| Number of City Development Plans (CDPs) appraised | 64 |
| Number of Memorandums of Agreement signed | 62 |
| Number of projects approved (till 28 August 2009) | 473 |
| Total approved project cost (for 473 projects) | Rs. 51,127.17 crore |
| Number of states for which projects approved (out of 31 states/UTs) | 30 |
| Number of cities for which projects approved (out of 65 cities) | 61 |
| Allocation for seven years (for UIG component) (ACA available as per original allocation) | Rs. 25,500 crore |
| Total ACA committed for 473 projects (original allocation-Rs. 21,704.66 crore, additional allocation-Rs. 2,531.69 crore) | Rs. 24,236.35 crore |
| Balance ACA available from the original allocation | Rs. 3,795.33 crore |
| ACA released for projects (till 25 September 2009) | Rs. 8,986.87 crore |
| Grand total of ACA for projects, reimbursement cost of CDPs, reimbursement cost of DPRs, CPF fund and e-governance | Rs. 9,000.50 crore |
| Number of completed projects | 43 |
| Number of e-governance projects approved | 6 |

*Source: www.jnnurm.nic.in/nurmurdweb/defaultud.aspx*

According to the JNNURM website (Table 6.1), since inception till August 2009, 473 projects have been sanctioned at an approved cost of Rs. 51,127.17 crore for 61 cities across 30 states. While sanctioning projects, priority has been accorded to sectors that directly benefit the common man and the urban poor, in water supply, sanitation and storm water drainage. A parallel scheme of Urban Infrastructure Development Scheme for Small and Medium Towns (UIDSSMT) for non-mission cities and towns was also launched in 2005-06 under JNNURM. Since inception till March 2009, a total of 747 projects have been sanctioned at an approved cost of Rs. 12,793.81 crore for 632 towns. For these, an additional Central assistance (ACA) of Rs. 10,311.76 crore has been sanctioned against which Rs. 5,820.71 crore has been released.

The Union Ministry of Urban Development has prescribed standardised service level indicators for four basic urban services (water supply, sewerage, solid waste management and stormwater drainage) for enabling cities to monitor, manage and improve their services delivery. The mission cities in particular are expected to keep these benchmarks in view while implementing projects under the Mission. A separate capacity building programme, Capacity Building Scheme for Urban Local Bodies (C-BULB), has been drawn up for municipal bodies not covered under JNNURM. This scheme works through financial support to the identified institutions/cities/states for various work such as setting up centres of excellence, addressing specific capacity gaps in areas such as urban planning, socioeconomic and environmental planning, municipal service delivery including water supply, sewerage and sanitation, solid waste management, financial management, urban transport, cost recovery and user charges, implementing capacity building programmes under the National Urban Sanitation Policy launched in November 2008, implementing municipal reforms like property tax reforms, accounting reforms, e-governance, PPP etc.

While it is true that too little time has elapsed to monitor progress of JNNURM or projects under it, it is not difficult to understand why funds are going a-begging. Nearly four years later, just over a third of the Central government funds allocated under the scheme have been utilised. In fact, the Ministry of Urban Development tells a very different story from the survey. Their statistics say only 43 out of the 463 projects sanctioned under the urban infrastructure and governance head have been completed. These projects have a total sanctioned cost of Rs. 49,743 crore, out of which the central assistance came to over Rs. 23,548 crore till July 2009. Only about Rs. 8,252 crore of this has been released so far for these projects.

This sorry state of affairs[3] is partly because the municipal bodies and the states have not followed up with their matching grants after the first central release and partly because of their inability to spend the money. The Mission was designed to offer resources to states to build their urban infrastructure while reforming the way cities are run. This would have involved, for instance, abolishing the laws and rules pertaining to

---

3.    "Few Takers for JNNURM", *Business Standard*, 6 July 2009, p.16.

## Table 6.2

### *JNNURM Reforms for Cities*

| **Mandatory Reforms** | |
|---|---|
| *Reforms* | *Cities which have accomplished Reforms* |
| E-governance set-up | Hyderabad, Vijayawada, Visakhapatnam, Ahmedabad, Rajkot, Surat, Greater Mumbai, Coimbatore, Madurai, Chennai, Kolkata |
| Shift to double entry accounting | Hyderabad, Vijayawada, Visakhapatnam, Ahmedabad, Rajkot, Surat, Shimla, Kochi, Thiruvananthapuram, Bangalore, Mysore, Bhopal, Indore, Ujjain, Nagpur, Greater Mumbai, Bhubaneswar, Jaipur, Coimbatore, Madurai, Chennai, Allahabad, Kolkata |
| Property tax – 85% coverage | Vadodara, Pune, Coimbatore, Madurai, Chennai, Hyderabad, Vijayawada, Visakhapatnam, Rajkot, Agra, Allahabad |
| Property tax – 90% collection efficiency | Hyderabad, Vijayawada, Visakhapatnam, Chandigarh, Pune, Coimbatore, Allahabad, Lucknow, Asansol |
| 100 % cost recovery – O&M for water supply | Visakhapatnam, Nashik, Pune, Greater Mumbai, Chennai, Madurai |
| 100 % cost recovery – SWM | Visakapatnam, Nashik, Greater Mumbai |
| Internal earmarking of funds for services to urban poor | Hyderabad, Vijayawada, Visakhapatnam, Chandigarh, Raipur, Ahmedabad, Rajkot, Surat, Vadodara, Faridabad, Kochi, Thiruvananthapuram, Bangalore, Mysore, Bhopal, Indore, Jabalpur, Ujjain, Nagpur, Nanded, Nashik, Pune, Greater Mumbai, Kohima, Amritsar, Bhubaneswar, Puri, Jaipur, Ajmer, Coimbatore, Madurai, Chennai, Dehradun, Haridwar, Nainital, Agra, Allahabad, Kanpur, Lucknow, Mathura, Meerut, Varanasi, Asansol, Kolkata. |
| **Optional Reforms** | |
| Introduction of property title certification system in ULBs | Chandigarh, Rajkot |
| Revision of building bylaws– streamlining the approval process | Hyderabad, Vijayawada, Visakhapatnam, Guwahati, Amritsar, Ludhiana, Jaipur, Ajmer, Ahmedabad, Rajkot, Surat, Vadodara, Bhopal, Indore, Nagpur, Nashik, Pune, Asansol, Kolkata |
| Revision of building bylaws– Mandatory | Hyderabad, Vijayawada, Visakhapatnam, Patna, Delhi |
| Rainwater harvesting in all buildings | Ahmedabad, Rajkot, Surat, Vadodara, Faridabad, Shimla, Kochi, Thiruvananthapuram, Bangalore, Mysore, Indore, Ujjain, Nagpur, Pune, Jaipur, Ajmer, Coimbatore, Madurai, Chennai, Dehradun, Agra, Allahabad, Kanpur, Lucknow, Mathura, Meerut, Varanasi, Asansol, Kolkata |
| Earmarking 25% developed land in all housing projects for EWS/LIG | Chandigarh, Ahmedabad, Rajkot, Surat, Vadodara, Jabalpur, Amritsar, Ludhiana, Jaipur, Ajmer |
| Simplifying legal and procedural framework for conversion of agricultural land for non- | Hyderabad, Vijayawada, Visakhapatnam, Ahmedabad, Rajkot, Surat, Vadodara, Kochi, Thiruvananthapuram, Bangalore, Mysore, Bhopal, Indore, Jabalpur, Ujjain, |

*contd...*

*...contd...*

| Reforms | Cities which have accomplished Reforms |
| --- | --- |
| agricultural purposes | Indore, Jaipur, Ajmer, Coimbatore, Madurai, Chennai, Asansol, Kolkata |
| Bylaws on reuse of recycled water | Hyderabad, Vijayawada, Visakhapatnam, Chandigarh, Delhi, Bangalore, Mysore, Pune, Coimbatore, Madurai, Chennai, Asansol, Kolkata |
| Encouraging PPP | Hyderabad, Vijayawada, Visakhapatnam, Guwahati, Raipur, Panaji, Ahmedabad, Rajkot, Surat, Vadodara, Kochi, Thiruvananthapuram, Bangalore, Mysore, Bhopal, Indore, Jabalpur, Ujjain, Nagpur, Nanded, Nashik, Pune, Greater Mumbai, Kohima, Amritsar, Bhubaneswar, Puri, Jaipur, Ajmer, Coimbatore, Madurai, Chennai, Agra, Allahabad, Kanpur, Lucknow, Mathura, Meerut, Varanasi, Asansol, Kolkata |
| Administrative reforms | Nashik, Madurai, Coimbatore, Chennai |
| Structural reforms | Mysore, Madurai, Coimbatore, Chennai |
| Introduction of computerised registration of land and property | Hyderabad, Vijayawada, Visakhapatnam, Ahmedabad, Rajkot, Surat, Vadodara, Shimla, Bangalore, Mysore, Nagpur, Nanded, Greater Mumbai, Jaipur, Coimbatore, Madurai, Chennai |
| **State Level Reforms** | |
| 74th CAA (Transfer 12th Schedule functions) | Andhra Pradesh, Bihar, Chhattisgarh, Gujarat, Kerala, Madhya Pradesh, Maharashtra, Tamil Nadu, Tripura, West Bengal |
| 74th CAA (Constitution of DPC) | Andhra Pradesh, Assam, Bihar, Chhattisgarh, Goa, Gujarat, Haryana, Himachal Pradesh, Kerala, Karnataka, Madhya Pradesh, Maharashtra, Odisha, Rajasthan, Tamil Nadu, Uttar Pradesh, West Bengal |
| 74th CAA (Constitution of MPC) | Andhra Pradesh, Gujarat, West Bengal |
| Transfer-City planning function | Assam, Chhattisgarh, Gujarat, Andhra Pradesh, Himachal Pradesh, Kerala, Madhya Pradesh, Maharashtra, Tamil Nadu, West Bengal |
| Transfer-Water supply & sanitation | Andhra Pradesh, Bihar, Chandigarh, Chhattisgarh, Gujarat, Haryana, Himachal Pradesh, Kerala, Madhya Pradesh, Maharashtra, Tamil Nadu, West Bengal |
| Reform in rent control | Karnataka, Manipur, Mizoram, Nagaland, Odisha, Rajasthan, West Bengal |
| Stamp duty rationalisation to 5% | Chandigarh, Goa, Gujarat, Jharkhand, Maharashtra, Puducherry, Sikkim, Tripura |
| Repeal of ULCRA | Andhra Pradesh, Arunachal Pradesh, Assam, Bihar, Chandigarh, Chhattisgarh, Goa, Gujarat, Haryana, Himachal Pradesh, Jammu & Kashmir, Kerala, Karnataka, Madhya Pradesh, Maharashtra, Manipur, Meghalaya, Mizoram, Nagaland, Puducherry, Punjab, Odisha, Rajasthan, Sikkim, Tamil Nadu, Tripura, Uttarakhand, Uttar Pradesh |
| Enacting community participation law | Andhra Pradesh, Assam, Gujarat |
| Enacting public disclosure law | Andhra Pradesh, Assam, Gujarat, Maharashtra, Tripura, Uttar Pradesh |

*Source:  www.jnnurm.nic.in/nurmurdweb/defaultud.aspx*

unrealistic land ceilings and rent control. But the scheme's progress in states has been patchy and uneven. Even the laggard states, such as Delhi which has neither repealed land ceilings nor abolished the monopoly of the state-owned Delhi Development Authority (DDA), have continued to secure Central grants. Maharashtra has repealed the Act, a little too late, because most of the land is already notified and has resulted in expensive and time-consuming litigation.

This confusion is of course compounded by the fact that virtually no state, reluctant to devolve power, has transferred the urban planning function to local bodies. A few states have adopted the mayor-in-council structure of city government, which is considered effective. If this is the challenge faced by the metros and the A-cities, the state of affairs in small towns is easily guessed.

The situation has led to a virtual deconstruction of the concept of local self-government in many areas. The introduction to an incentive scheme[4] for *panchayats* in Himachal Pradesh says, somewhat contrarily, "The weak financial position of the Panchayats and their non-performance of statutory functions is creating the misconception in the rural areas that the *panchayats* are not a unit of self governance but is an agent of the State government. This is the major challenge for the Panchayati Raj system for which *State intervention* is required. One of the steps towards this direction can be to encourage the PRIs to generate their own resources and perform their statutory functions by providing incentive to them."

## Approaching the Market

With the introduction of the economic reforms and decentralised governance in the country, capital market borrowing, privatisation, partnership arrangements and community-based projects have emerged as favoured options for undertaking infrastructural investments and provision of basic amenities. Planners and policymakers have, in recent years, made a strong case to make the parastatal agencies as also the local governments depend increasingly on their internal resources and institutional finance with the objective of "bringing in efficiency and accountability in their

---

4.  Scheme for Availing Incentive against the Net Fresh Additional Resource Mobilisation by *Gram Panchayats*, Ministry of Panchayati Raj, Government of Himachal Pradesh, August 2008.

functioning." To address the fiscal stress, some ULBs began resorting to borrowings in recent years, often with state government guarantees, from Housing and Urban Development Corporation (HUDCO), financial institutions, banks, the open market, and external lending agencies like the World Bank and the Asian Development Bank.

In a paper on financing needs of Asian urbanisation over the next 30 years, former RBI deputy governor Rakesh Mohan (2006) notes interestingly that financial markets in Asia have not been sophisticated enough to allow for borrowing from the credit or bond markets as in case of Europe or North America. Financing of urban infrastructure in Asia is usually done by national governments who raise resources from taxes, or from banks and financial institutions that have been typically government owned or sponsored. As cities gradually develop self-sustaining local taxation and user fees so that they can tap national and international financial markets, urbanisation of Asia in the coming years will put pressure on international resource mobilisation and will in turn get reflected in higher interest rates.

**Figure 6.2**

*Municipal Financing through Non-Conventional Resources*

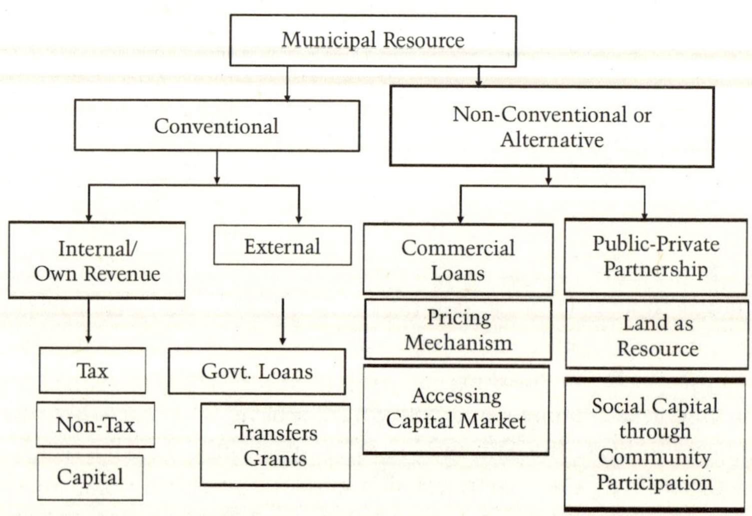

Given their poor financial position, the ULBs are not able to raise loans or issue bonds from either the financial institutions or the market without state government guarantees. That is understandable, since according to Mathur and Ray (2003), as of 31 March 2001, the state governments had accumulated contingent liabilities of Rs. 5,250 crore on behalf of the municipalities. This is particularly relevant in the context of some of the state governments, which are increasing their own outstanding liabilities by directly assuming the responsibility for repaying the loans taken by urban local bodies from external lending agencies. Kerala has done this.

By law, the state governments can not only guarantee repayment but they can specify for what projects municipal bodies can resort to borrowing, these being: a) construction of permanent works, b) acquisition of lands and buildings, c) paying off any debt due to government, and d) repaying loan previously raised under municipal and other laws. The states also prescribe conditions regarding security, rate of interest, repayment of principal and interest, date of floatation and time schedule for loan repayment. Such borrowing restrictions need to be relaxed if the lenders have to depend on the market or guided by pre-specified principles.

Some key options for financing urban infrastructure include: i) specialised banks for municipal lending, as used in western Europe, ii) municipal bond markets as in North America, and iii) specialised municipal funds an example of which is the Tamil Nadu Urban Development Fund.

For accessing capital market funds, Bagchi (2001) argues, municipalities need financial, structural, institutional and administrative changes. These include: i) placing certain buoyant revenue sources at their disposal, ii) transforming the urban governance system with limited control by state governments, iii) changing the capital market structure, iv) recovering the cost of services, and v) escrowing mechanisms to make the urban infrastructure projects commercially viable.

One of the first efforts by municipal bodies in India in raising public money was the Rs. 100 crore bonds issue by Ahmedabad Municipal Corporation (AMC) in early 1998; and Vaidya and Johnson (2001) suggest that the technical framework developed in this case act as a blueprint for future development initiatives in this area. The first such instrument issued without any state guarantee, it marked the first tentative step towards market-based local government finance. The AMC first introduced reforms to improve revenue collection to make up for the loss it had been incurring and prepared a five-year capital investment or corporate plan and credit rating by the CRISIL. For debt servicing, revenues from 10 octroi collection centres were placed in an escrow account-structured debt obligation (SDO). Other credit enhancing measures adopted by the AMC were fixing minimum average debt service coverage ratio of 1.5 and having a sinking fund for repayment of principal and mortgage equal to 1.2 times the par value of the bonds.

Nashik Municipal Corporation too raised Rs. 150 million through two kinds of bonds—taxable bonds for Rs. 100 and taxfree ones for Rs. 50 with a coupon rate of 7.75 per cent, some 250 basis points higher than a comparative maturity government paper. Both the bonds had been assigned 'AA(So)' by CRISIL based on the corporation's strong standalone credit quality and credit enhancement mechanisms provided for in the form of an escrow of the corporation's revenue streams. The revenues were expected to flow from increased octroi collections and lower capital expenditure on the Kumbh festival and the Godavari Action Plan.

Spurred on by JNNURM, credit rating of ULBs has been undertaken in the mission cities to facilitate leveraging of debt for urban infrastructure projects. Of the 58 ULBs which have been assigned draft ratings, 36 have investment grade credit rating. Under the Pooled Finance Development Fund (PFDF) Scheme, which is expected to provide more credit to ULBs so that they can access market borrowings through state-level pooled finance mechanism, eight states have set up their "State Pooled Finance Entity" as per guidelines. The first proposal for issue of tax-free Pooled Finance Development Bond worth Rs. 45 crore by Water and Sanitation Pooled Fund, the designated instrument of Tamil Nadu, was notified and appropriate releases towards the Fund and project development cost were made in February 2008.

**Table 6.3**

*Bonds Issues by Municipal Bodies in India*

| City | Amount (Rs. million) | Interest % | Escrow Arrangement | Purpose | Credit Rating |
|---|---|---|---|---|---|
| Ahmedabad | 1000 | 14 | Octroi from 10 octroi collection points | Water supply & sewerage project | AA-(SO) |
| Bangalore | 1250 | 13 | State government grants and property tax | City roads/ street drains | A-(SO) |
| Ludhiana | 100 | 13.5 to 14 | Water and sewerage taxes and charges | Water supply & sewerage project | LAA-(SO) |
| Nagpur | 500 | 13 | Property tax and water charges | Water supply & sewerage project | LAA-(SO) |
| Nashik | 1000 | 14.75 | Octroi from 4 octroi collection points | Water supply & sewerage project | AA-(SO) |
| Indore | 100 | | NA | Improvement of city roads | A(SO) |
| Madurai | 300 | 12.25 | Toll tax collection | City road project | LA+(SO) |
| Ahmedabad (tax free) | 1000 | 9 | Property taxes of 2 zones | Water supply & sewerage project | AA(SO) |
| Hydrabad (tax free) | 825 | 8.5 | Non-residential property tax, advertisement tax,professional tax, etc. | Road construction and widening | LAA+(SO) AA+(SO) |
| Tamil Nadu (pooled financing) | 110 | 9.20 | Monthly payments equal to one-ninth of their annual payments | Water supply & sewerage project in 14 MCs | LAA(SO) |

*Source:* Mathur (2006).

Mathur (2006) says that the example of the "successful cases of pooled finance in Tamil Nadu and Karnataka show that the mechanism offers a viable option for the financing" of urban infrastructure in small and medium ULBs. With support from Financial Institutions Reform and Expension-Debt (FIRE-D), Tamil Nadu developed a Rs. 30.41 crore pooled bond issue with USAID Development Credit Authority guarantee, whose proceeds would fund water and sewerage projects in 14 small and medium sized towns in the Chennai metro area. The bond has a 9.20 per cent annual interest rate, 15-year maturity, redemption in 15 equal annual instalments and can be put/called at the end of 10 years. The bonds were signed a credit rating of Ind AA (SO) by Fitch and LAA (SO) by ICRA. While the bonds were unsecured, a multi-layered credit enhancement mechanism was set up. The bond was privately placed with five domestic investors in December 2002. The small water and sewerage projects in the 14 ULBs are complete and repayment is proceeding as per the pooled finance structure.

The FIRE-D project also supported the government of Karnataka in the financial structuring of a Rs. 659 crore water and sewerage project that utilises the pooled finance mechanism. The project will bring potable water and waterborne sewerage for the first time to 1.2 million inhabitants living in eight smaller ULBs surrounding Bangalore city. These rapidly growing areas are home to Bangalore's burgeoning information technology and more recently, biotechnology and genetic engineering industry. The state mobilised Rs. 100 crore from the domestic capital markets in June 2005 to partly fund the water component of the project, apart from going in for a USAID-DCA agreement with built-in credit enhancement to reduce the cost of borrowing for the eight ULBs. The tax-free bond has tenure of 15 years, three year moratorium on principal with repayment beginning from the fourth year, and an annual interest rate of 5.95 per cent. The issue, rated LAA (SO) by ICRA, was placed privately with 13 investors. As with the Tamil Nadu pooled bond, a multi-layered credit enhancement mechanism was set up.

Beyond these examples, however, as the Economic Survey says, "the progress of the scheme has been slow and the current downturn in global and national finances is not helping." Also, such alternatives have not been useful for small and medium towns, which usually have a much higher percentage of households not having access to basic amenities along with fewer fiscal reform options.

The danger of external finance is that getting into long-term debt servicing may make the cities financially vulnerable. This is where the state government needs to step in. They have not only to ensure the autonomy of the local bodies and their capacity to take up essential services as well as slum improvement and social development projects but also watch out for conditionalities imposed by credit rating agencies and other financial intermediaries that may hamper such services. The SFCs may recommend specific grants, tied to provision of services to poor and slum colonies.

# Areas of Reforms in ULBs

Of late, several state governments and municipalities have embarked upon initiatives to increase their revenue base. Such initiatives have revolved around a few core ones such as, property tax reforms involving a shift from annual ratable value to a unit area system, substitution of cash-based to an accrual-based accounting system, forging a better linkage between price (tariff) and cost of services, and public-private partnerships in service provision. But these initiatives have had limited coverage and success because of a host of constraints—stagnating revenues, weak political and administrative leadership, experimentation with alternative modes and so on.

The reform roadmap for ULBs relies on two critical internal reforms: discovering "lost income" through financial management and discovering "lost performance" through performance orientation. Often, it is easier to quickly turn around a local body than a large corporation. Several municipal governments have undertaken certain financial reforms in the following areas, some of which are very progressive and impressive though not always very successful.

- Property Tax Reforms.
- Introduction of Double Entry Accounting System.
- E-Governance (using IT, GIS and MIS).
- Computerisation of Municipal Records.
- User Charges and Services to the Urban Poor.

## Property Tax Reform

Land-based taxes is considered by all as the most appropriate sources of local body finances, especially in the case of developing countries like India where the local authorities are required to provide the basic civic infrastructure facilities. This is mainly because property tax is both a tax and an incentive. Efficient local government spending translates into better infrastructure, better functioning cities and towns and rapid urbanisation, all of which in turn leads to rising land values. The land-owners benefit proportionately more than what they pay as taxes, leading to agglomeration economies.

The OECD's Centre for Tax Policy and Administration periodically publishes statistical data and analytical papers on inter-governmental finances of OECD and non-OECD countries. Studies relating to OECD countries (see Annexure Table A-1.5) reveal that property tax is the dominant local tax in Australia, Canada, Ireland, New Zealand, the UK and the US. Even these countries have either less important local governments, as in Ireland and Australia, or local governments that are more dependent on inter-governmental transfers such as Canada and the UK. Income tax is the most important local tax in nine countries—Austria, Belgium, Luxembourg, Switzerland, Norway, Sweden, Denmark, Finland and Japan. A few, such as France, Spain, Portugal, Italy and Turkey, have a balanced local tax structure. However, in majority of these countries, as opposed to India, property taxes seldom accounted for more than 20 per cent of local current revenues.

Several researchers have highlighted how Indian municipalities have not succeeded in realising the potential of the property tax, though property values are climbing rapidly. A major problem with the property tax system in India lies in the process of tax computation. The linking of the property tax based on annual rental value (ARV) with the rent control law has hindered the growth of collection. In case of property tax, the introduction of capital value assessment system should be a longer term objective, though the system is difficult and costly to implement. Area-based property tax system, based on a self-assessment scheme, holds promise.

Most city governments have undertaken the property tax reforms both from the administrative and taxpayer's perspectives. These include Ahmedabad, Bhopal, Indore, Patna, Lucknow, Mirzapur, Thiruvananthapuram, Bangalore and Hyderabad. The areas of reform are mostly related to tax administration, tax structure and related legal issues and policy and institutional issues. The Bangalore experience needs to be detailed.

Property tax is the only major tax that the Bruhat Bengaluru Mahanagara Palike (BMP) (Bangalore Metropolitan Authority) is authorised to collect under the Karnataka Municipal Corporation Act, 1976. The revenue department in the BMP, entrusted with the job of assessing the properties and collecting the tax has 1086 personnel (officers, assessors, inspectors, collectors, etc.), considered by the citizens as the most corrupt in the organisation. In 2000, the BNP introduced an optional scheme of self-assessment of property tax "without amending the municipal act or the rules." The method of assessment was based on 4 parameters: location of the building (estimated market value of the land notified by the government under Section 45-B of the Karnataka Stamp Act, 1957 as per 6 zones created based on the guidance value); type of construction (capital cost of construction); age of the building (depreciation factor); and status (usage factor) of tenancy and self-occupation, with a 50 per cent rebate for the latter. The scheme also envisaged 5 per cent scrutiny of the self-assessment declaration received. By amendments to the KMN Act in 2001 and 2003, the entire property tax system has been changed from estimation at annual rental value basis to capital value system, while self-assessment of the capital value and the tax payable by the owner of the property has been retained.

## Fiscal and Administration Reforms

Strengthening, streamline and simplification of the tax machinery is a must to check tax evasion and promote tax compliance. It will also help to improve the business environment. Moreover, improved management of expenditure will ensure more efficient use of scarce funds and reduce unproductive and wasteful expenditure on one hand and improve the quality of expenditure on the other by protecting capital expenditure and maintenance. This will entail reforms in budgeting, accounting, internal control and audit, cash and debt management and management information system.

## Accounting Reforms

The first State Finance Commission of Rajasthan[5] said in its report in 1995: "A comparison of the income and expenditure for 1993-94 for individual category of ULBs, though shows a surplus, the reality is different (*sic*). The ULBs have devised a system for financing these activities by diverting employees PF/pension amount to other heads of expenditure.....It is clear that the apparent category-wise surplus position reflected by the ULBs do not reflect the truth and in reality, the municipalities at all levels have deficit because of their default on deposition of Provident Fund/ Pension amount."

---

5.  Government of Rajasthan (1995). *Report of the First State Finance Commission (1995-2000)*. December. Jaipur. p.227.

Municipalities are statutorily required to maintain a balanced budget and in several states, even a surplus. But because they have a cash-based accounting system and an absence of distinction between capital account and revenue account receipts and expenditures, it becomes near impossible to track and incorporate outstanding payments. Several municipal bodies do not pay back their dues to the state governments and thus manage to post large surpluses even when their accounts are in the red, as the Rajasthan SFC pointed out.

The NASSCOM report of July 2006, "E-Governance Accelerating, but Roadblocks Exist", estimates that in the next five years, state governments in India will spend close to Rs. 15,000 crore on computerising their operations.[6] The pressure to be IT-savvy is not only to keep up with the times but emerges from pragmatism. Loans to governments from multilaterals have now become more or less contingent upon a proper treasury management system which translates into a computerised system that can tell lending institutions what has happened to the money that it has lent.

## Services Reform

A good example of services reform is the Rs. 745 crore six-year Andhra Pradesh Urban Services for the Poor (APUSP) Project, an innovative partnership project between the state government and the government of UK (project cost is a grant from DFID), being implemented in the 32 Class 1 towns of the state, to achieve improved access to more appropriate and sustainable services for the urban poor, specifically 2.2 million slum dwellers. It focuses on municipal reform: improved financial, planning and implementation capabilities of the municipal towns; improvement of environmental infrastructure in urban slums including water supply, sanitation, solid waste management, drainage, roads/ footpaths, street lights, etc., and envisages working with civil society in order to enhance the range and quality of services and initiatives for the poor through participatory planning.

---

6.   KPMG-CII Connect (2009). *Resurgence of Indian ICT Sector*. 10-12 September, *Chennai in.kpmg.com*

## Public-Private Partnership

Most of the SFCs have laid great emphasis on public-private partnership. Such participation, they advocated, would offer new techniques, lead to improvement in operational efficiency, being potentially new sources of finance. While the advantage in terms of raising revenue may not be very big, non-monetary gains could outweigh the monetary gains. Such non-monetary gains may come about in the form of better utilisation of labour force, improved delivery of civic services leading to greater interest and involvement of the public in civic affairs, putting greater pressure on municipal administration and the elected representatives in discharging their duties and functions. Most of the SFCs have also identified common areas where public participation would pay dividends. These areas include, street lighting, sanitation, public health, solid waste management, maintenance of water system, billing and collection of taxes, road construction and maintenance, maintenance of parks and gardens, playing grounds and swimming pools, social forestry, reading of meters, maintenance and operation of tube wells, etc.

According to Bagchi (2001), who analysed the nitty-gritty of alternative/unconventional modes of financing urban infrastructure, the objective of public-private partnership relates much more to attracting capital and curtailing public sector employment than increasing the efficiency and effectiveness of service delivery. He ascribes the failure of the PPP model to two factors: the lack of customer approach in it, and the extensive focus on technical and commercial aspects of infrastructure.

Still, since PPPs are getting popular, it is important to watch out for certain unhealthy developments. At the city level, it is important to ensure that inequalities do not rise due to location of infrastructural projects by dint of eviction or displacement or due to contractual agreements for service delivery. This can make private companies lose interest as has indeed happened in water supply and solid waste management, and show interest only in O&M jobs. Specific clauses must be built in the new capital projects and contractual agreements with these private agencies so that the neglected populace is no further neglected. Also, government projects must be taken up alongside to take care of the slums and poor colonies, for implementation with subsidy and within a participatory framework. The

ULBs must realise that equity in basic services is a basic tenet in their existence, or made to realise with penal provisions for failing to meet this obligation.

## Municipal Bodies at Crossroads

It is clear from the discussions so far that not only are finances of the local governments in India in tatters but their limited fiscal powers preclude any possibility of a radical improvement in the situation. The resource crunch and fiscal stress faced by them does not augur well for an equitable and adequate delivery of municipal services to large numbers of people. Poor tax administration, management and collection procedure have helped to keep the share of own revenues in total municipal income low as well as the per capita spending level below established norms. As the PRIA survey shows, the situation is much more serious in the small and medium towns of the country where revenue collection from domestic sources is low and the flow of revenues from non-tax sources is erratic and unpredictable and establishment costs are alarmingly high. Even the external finance options utilised by the big cities and metros are not a plausible alternative for them. All these factors have conspired to keep them overwhelmingly dependent on their respective governments and the degree of dependence can even go up to more than 80 per cent as in the case of Rajasthan.

What then is the way out? While JNNURM, comprising a series of reforms, such as property tax reform, introduction of double entry accounting system, better user charges, e-governance etc., was launched as a panacea, the response to it has been at best lukewarm. As for SFC recommendations, the enormous delay in submission of action taken reports and the implementation of these recommendations by state governments slow down the process of fiscal decentralisation and defeat the purpose of setting up SFCs. Many governments have also ignored or delayed implementing the financial recommendations for municipal governments, while recommendations related to devolution have been either partially accepted or sometimes wholly rejected.

Yet, such a situation does not seem practicable anymore. Increasing urbanisation, migration from rural areas and the latest delimitation of parliamentary and assembly constituencies have raised the size as well as clout of urban voters. This process will gather momentum as delimitation is now slated to take place every decade. The 2009 delimitation, for instance, raised the number of Lok Sabha constituencies from 70 to more than 100. Keeping this in view, the 13th Finance Commission has tried to redefine the existing structure of fiscal federalism by giving local bodies a direct share in Union tax revenues, bypassing the state governments.

The report recommended that the share of urban local bodies *vis-à-vis* rural ones be raised from the current 1:4 in tune with their population growth *vis-à-vis* rural bodies. Raising the state share in Union tax revenues from 30.5 per cent to 32 per cent, it called for a 2.5 per cent share (1 per cent share to be based on performance) of the divisible pool for local bodies in the form of grants, as the Constitution does not allow the sharing of tax revenues with them. This provision will hopefully allow competition among states to utilise Central funds more effectively.

Stressing that inclusive growth requires a "fiscally strong Centre, states as well as third tier (local bodies)," the report also lays emphasis on state-specific grants on the basis of fiscal needs, fiscal capacity and the relative cost of providing similar levels of public goods and services. Interestingly, the government has declared to have accepted most of these recommendations.

Reforms that go beyond the fiscal package are more significant. Releasing their significance, the 12th Finance Commission had recommended devolution of funds to the states for two specific purposes, reform in the system of accounting of local bodies and the need for building up database. None of these have happened yet. In the next and the concluding chapter, we discuss the well-known financial and administrative solutions as well as the possibility of finding ways and means that complement and yet go beyond the fiscal package to help municipal bodies play their true role in the Indian federal democracy.

## Table 6.4

### *An Inventory of Urban Initiatives*[7]

| Initiative | City |
| --- | --- |
| Community participation for effective solid waste management | Hyderabad, Mumbai, Tirupur |
| Modified accrual based accounting system | Hyderabad |
| E-governance using cable network | Vijaywada |
| E-governance initiative | Vishakhapatnam |
| Public-private partnership in | |
| City greening | Visakhapatnam |
| Slum networking | Ahmedabad |
| River cleaning | Kodinar |
| Street light maintenance | Bangalore, Jaipur |
| Development of compost plant | Puri |
| Street intersection maintenance | Jodhpur, Rudrapur |
| Solid waste management | Pune |
| Sustained resource mobilisation strategies | Ahmedabad |
| Heritage conservation initiative | Ahmedabad |
| Town planning scheme | Ahmedabad |
| Monitoring system for performance management | Surat |
| Energy efficient street lighting system | Vadodara |
| Municipal debt management | Vadodara |
| Revitalisation of the city lake | Navsari |
| Bio-composting of solid waste | Valsad |
| Innovations in municipal budgeting and financial management | Bangalore |
| Wireless grievances redress system | Tumkur, Mumbai |
| Mobilisation of financial resources | Indore |
| Sanitation facilities for slum dwellers | Mumbai |
| Strategy for reducing unaccounted for water | Nagpur |
| Integrated development of urban roads | Nagpur |
| Advanced water billing at reduced rates | Thane |
| Lakefront development on BOT basis | Coimbatore |
| Development of electric cremation with community based orgs. | Tirupur |
| Comprehensive solid waste management strategy | Tirupur |
| People's participation in underground sewerage | Alandur |
| Zero garbage town | Namakkal |
| Public-private partnership in solid waste management | Rudrapur |
| Computerisation of building plan sanction | Mussoorie |
| Birth-death registration system | Dehradun |

*Source:* City Managers' Association Gujarat (2003). *Best Practices Catalogue 2002.* Ahmedabad, Gujarat.

---

7.   Mathur and Thakur (2004).

7

# Beyond the Fiscal Package

*Local Governments as
Executive Stakeholders*

Democratic decentralisation is welcome because it not only helps to correct the distortions caused by the abuse of power of public agencies and make them more accountable but also makes these agencies more responsive, participative and transparent. Transparency facilitates participation and participation makes a public agency really responsive to people's needs.

In order that local bodies (*panchayats* and municipalities) can grow and develop as a third tier of governance, the National Commission set up to review the working of the Constitution of India recommended on 31 March 2002, as necessary conditions that: a) municipalities should have a set of exclusive functions, and b) the concept of a distinct and separate tax domain for municipalities should be recognised.[1] If this were to happen, the basic character of the Constitution would change with major implications for inter-governmental relations.

As long as this radical solution is not implemented, the way forward for municipalities has to come out of the existing system of governance. But self-reliance and autonomy at the local level cannot be simply achieved by Constitutional amendment. For that, there is a strong need for internal reforms to break the vicious cycle of poor finances and performances as well as evolving a partnership between the stakeholders in urban governance, the local bodies and the public to bring about effective and efficient delivery of local urban services. A whole host of measures are required that go beyond the fiscal package.

## Making SFCs Serve Local Bodies

The first area in this respect is SFCs. Improving the way they are set up and made to give their recommendations and making it mandatory for

---

1. *http://lawmin.nic.in/ncrwc/ncrwcreport.htm*

state governments to implement those suggestions can help ULBs a great deal. From the experience of the SFCs so far, it is possible to conclude that:

- State governments have not made any genuine effort to make clear expenditure assignments to the local bodies and also restructure their own setup.

- State government staff transfers to the local bodies have not been accompanied by revenue source transfers.

- SFCs waste a lot of time in collecting financial data from the local bodies, which should otherwise have been collected as a matter of routine through an in-built system. Collection of qualitative data in vital areas such as fiscal autonomy/revenue dependence, expenditure/revenue decentralisation has not been attempted so far.

- SFCs are supposed to recommend fiscal transfers to add to local revenues and not give finance for creating local infrastructure. This fact is little known.

- SFCs have not paid much attention to improve fiscal administration of local bodies. This might be more important that fiscal transfers *per se*.

- SFCs are not required to cover issues of local taxation or borrowings; in case some of these are required to be examined 'in the interest of sound finance', these should be specifically included in their terms of reference.

- SFCs did not begin their work by reviewing state finances first; nor did they suggest significant transfer of or levying a surcharge on state taxes.

- SFCs have neglected the adverse consequences of grants on local revenue efforts and local fiscal autonomy.

- State governments treat the SFCs with scant respect, partly due to their membership composition that includes serving civil servants, and

- Delayed acceptance of and acting upon the SFCs recommendations must stop. Also, as in the case of CFCs, SFC recommendations must be binding on governments.

Also, transfer of finances should be linked to outcomes rather than to outputs. Joshi and Ray (2005) say that a focus on outcomes rather than outputs warrants more autonomy in the hands of the local body that would be used to achieve the set outcomes. One of the instruments for ensuring an outcome orientation to fiscal transfers is to devolve greater amount of funds as unspecified grants (untied funds) which could be used to meet the overall socioeconomic objectives of the municipal bodies. Kerala, which has allocated greater amount of funds in this form, has been able to accomplish better outcomes than Karnataka where the transfer of funds is for much more specific purposes even though the proportion of state revenues transferred in both the cases is roughly the same.

## Breaking the Vicious Cycle of Poor Finances and Performance

### Emerging Reform Issues for Municipal Bodies

Before going into the non-fiscal alternatives, let us summarise the important fiscal, administrative and political recommendations that have come out of the study towards an efficient performance by the municipal network in India.[2]

- Reforms have to be initiated so that in the long term, the municipal bodies emerge financially self-sufficient. Revenue assignment must be clear and revenue assignment must correspond to expenditure assignment.

- Tax reforms should be initiated to expand tax base, improve tax collection, particularly property tax collection.

- User charges and fees should be levied at more realistic and cost-effective rates to help consolidate non-tax incomes.

- Involve private operators in the tax administration, especially in tax collection with regular follow-up and monitoring system.

- Initiate legal reforms to reduce the gaps between arrears and actual collection of taxes.

---

2. A few of these recommendations have been reiterated by the Thirteenth Finance Commission.

- The inter-governmental transfer system must be urgently reformed. Given the limitations to increasing own sources, there is a strong case for institutionalising resource flow from the higher level of governments to ULBs, especially transfers from states, based on a set of principles and incentives, replacing the current ad hoc system with very little incentive to ULBs for bridging fiscal gap and improving service quality.

- Disbursal of revenue grants to the municipalities should be undertaken as and when necessary. The SFCs need to continue with such recommendations. At the same time, it should impose fiscal responsibility norms to ensure that receipt of adequate revenue grants does not mean that municipal bodies do not have any incentive to mobilise own resources and help create a culture of bailouts.

- Establishment expenditures are very high and can singlehandedly bring about a crisis in the finances of municipalities in a poor revenue year. But since such expenditures are steady and recurrent in the government, they are not easy to curtail. Still, municipalities must try and minimise establishment expenditure and restrict its growth, especially in non-essential areas. For instance, there is usually an excess of clerical/bureaucratic staff in municipalities, who are arbitrarily appointed without adhering to any norms of staffing structure, and here such austerity measures can be applied. However, this directive should not apply to components of establishment expenditures that directly contribute to basic services, such as the salaries of sweepers, staff of health centres and primary school teachers.

- For development, most of the small and medium towns of India need more capital resources and bottlenecks in the way of spending on capital development should be identified and cleared. Meticulous accounts must be kept of capital receipts and expenditures. For the present, more capital grants would be needed as these small towns are not yet creditworthy.

- Recovery of advances and refund of deposits should be more efficient. All inflows and outflows relating to the extraordinary account should be meticulously recorded.

- In prioritising expenditure, the right balance needs to be struck. For instance, while it is important to spend on public works, other functions such as running clinics and hospitals for slums should not be neglected.

- Major structural reforms in accounting and financial management of municipal bodies are needed. Of utmost urgency is the need to initiate accounting reforms at municipal bodies to help them prepare better and meticulous budgets and facilitate accurate financial reporting. Accrual-based accounting must be put in place following the National Municipal Accounting Manual. Municipal accounts may be disclosed to the public at regular intervals in simple and easily understandable formats to induce informed debate and enforce vigilance. Consistent record keeping towards achieving a uniform practice of financial data entry formats and procedures in all states should be the target.

- Capacity building of urban local bodies, specially in the smaller and medium towns is important as is unbundling of services.

- Raising the general rates of tariff to a level that a small surplus is generated to cross-subsidise programmes in slum colonies, besides meeting their O&M costs.

- Relaxation in conditions of various international and national level financial-cum-development agencies in view of the special situation of small and medium towns and also slum colonies within large cities, while financing infrastructural projects.

- The role of parastatals should be debated and revised, with the objective of more autonomy to local governments.

- The fiscal position of the country is now analysed with respect to the combined fiscal deficit, that is, the finances of Central and state governments only. To get a comprehensive idea about the country's fiscal situation, it is essential to consider the finances of local bodies as Constitutional entities in their own right supplying a variety of civic amenities and infrastructure. Ideally, state governments should do it, but to begin with, the RBI should at least initiate this exercise in the same way as it does for the states.

- Delink local initiatives from political motives through involvement of community.

- Civil society organisations should spearhead the cause of mobilising more effective citizens' participation in urban governance, awareness among citizens of various components of municipal services and governance, and allow for expression of citizens' needs.

- Include the local people in the budget preparation process for the appropriate funds allocation. This is a must because residents have a better understanding of the magnitude of the problems in their areas and may come up with better and more practicable solutions which can be more easily implemented through their participation.

---

**Box 7.1**

*Recommendations in a Nutshell*

**Financial**
- Better tax collection through property tax reforms.
- Consolidating incomes from fees and user charges by more realistic rates.
- Continuing revenue grants till municipalities are more self-sufficient.
- Imposing fiscal responsibility.
- Checking growth of establishment expenditures.
- Augment capital resources for development.
- Refund deposits and recover advances efficiently.
- Ensure balanced spending on all functions.

**Institutional**
- Initiate accounting reforms on a war footing.
- Revise the role of parastatal bodies.
- Reform inter-governmental transfer system.

**Civil Society**
- Build platform for citizens' participation.
- Create awareness among citizens on rights, responsibilities and equity.
- Transparent functioning and e-governance facilitates involvement from all quarters.

---

## Citizens Participation in Urban Governance

### Neither in Letter Nor Spirit

Public-private partnerships may assume different forms, varying from contracting out municipal services to the private sector, participation of private sector in the creation and operation of civic services and the involvement of voluntary groups in the implementation of programmes. It is the third area that has seen radical evolution in recent times, leading to major improvement in service delivery.

**Box 7.2**

Citizens have no direct participation. Representation is through Elected Representatives, who are most of the time not sensitive to the needs of citizens. They show apathy to the problems in their municipalities. Even the bureaucrats involved in ULBs are disparaging about the abilities of the elected representatives.

To involve local communities in some of the tasks allotted to ULBs, the 74th CAA envisages area *sabhas* and ward committees similar to the *gram sabhas* in villages. However, in most small towns, this form of public participation has not taken root. The towns in the PRIA survey, for instance, did not yield any evidence of direct citizens' participation, particularly in planning and budget-making processes, other than indirect participation through representatives. The ward councillors are expected to incorporate the demands and wants of the citizens during budget preparation and other matters of urban governance but seldom do. Except in some towns in Haryana, councillors are neither approachable nor sensitive to the needs of the citizens. In some places, as in Himachal Pradesh, NGOs do provide support and platform for expression of citizens' problems and needs but this is by no means extensive.

The citizens too reciprocate by expressing utter apathy to the governance of their city. During this study, citizens were randomly approached and interviewed. In each town, citizens from all socioeconomic groups were targeted and despite their apathy, they expressed strong views. Most of them said they were not averse to paying taxes and all other charges for municipal services, provided that they saw those services being delivered. They didn't seem to realise that was a chicken-and-egg syndrome and therefore a short-sighted approach. On the whole, however, they were unanimous in demanding better solid waste management in the city, more streetlights, better and more roads and efficient sewerage. In Himachal Pradesh, they voiced the need to build children's playgrounds, which is rare to come by in this hilly terrain.

Elected women representatives in the towns studied are mostly non-functional and figureheads; the male relatives, mostly spouses, perform or dictate the official duties. A 2006 study by NIUA revealed that not only were 87 per cent of them elected for the first time, two-thirds were also just housewives.[3] Many women are never told that they need to attend meetings. In Janjgir, the husband of the woman councillor had given up his business to devote himself full-time to the work which his wife was to do. The only exception is Haryana where the women are more vocal and active. While women representatives are aware of this failing and their slow progress in the political arena, they aver that without reservation of seats for women in urban local body elections, even this much might not be there.

To explore how well citizens are participating in urban governance, PRIA conducted semi-structured interviews of municipal officers (elected councillors and executive staff) as well as residents from different socio-economic backgrounds, which threw up some interesting findings.[4]

In most of the towns, municipal officers took the stand that they were doing their best within logistical, financial and political constraints. They also felt that the general condition of the town was alright and citizens were adequately represented in running services. By contrast, citizens were vocally dissatisfied with the provision of basic services, which they said was neither enough nor okay, and they also felt totally ignored and excluded by the urban governance process.

There are several reasons for this wide divide among the administrators and the administered. Elected councillors not only did not think from the citizen's point of view but, after winning the municipal election, did not even bother to implement what the citizens wanted. Priorities were determined by a host of factors that might or might not be cognizant of citizens' needs. Most vital functions, such as budget preparation or town planning, were not shared with them, partly because of the general perception among municipal bodies that citizens wouldn't 'understand' the issues. This belief is partly true. Most of the citizens (educated and uneducated) do not have a systematic understanding of

---

3.   NIUA (2006).

4.   Ray (2007).

urban governance and its constraints or do not know how to express and fight for their needs and therefore, suffer from unrealistic expectations and a sense of cynicism. It is possible to bridge the gap between the two groups by sustained communication about needs and constraints but that does not exist at present.

Also, the presence of political loyalties/priorities and local corruption erodes from within the cause of accountable and participatory local governance. Three patterns emerge. First, the elected representative generally does not care about the citizen's needs and is following his/her own vested interests, whether political or personal. In a Himachal Pradesh town, the councillors were alleged to be using municipal resources to build their own properties. The second problem was domination by the chairman of the board, who did not listen to the more honest elected colleagues and those who actually thought of citizens. The chairman of a small town municipal body in Uttar Pradesh, with a dangerous criminal record, held sway over all other elected representatives, citizens and even state officials and police, and acted like a dictator. The third instance of subversion of citizens' participation occurred at the executive staff level, where there is low regard for the wishes of the citizens or even their elected representatives. Some elected representatives in some towns of Chhattisgarh are effectively kept out of the budget process, as they are called only at the final stage for the sake of quorum and formality.

Thus, civil society organisations need to engage more with urban citizens and generate better awareness of civic and governance issues. The need of the hour is a common platform where citizens and municipal officers may express their needs and constraints, in an ongoing dialogue. This would foster a team spirit and build the foundation of effective and direct citizens' participation in the future. The area *sabha* or *mohalla samitis* may be a good starting point, as illustrated by PRIA's work in Jhunjhunu (see Box 7.3).

Here, the role of civil society organisations (CBOs and NGOs) assumes crucial importance as mediator, watchdog, informer, facilitator and enabler. At present, the civil society organisations working in urban governance face several challenges, while engaging with the different tiers in the society: with government and policymakers for demanding effective decentralisation, with councillors while informing, sensitising and mobilising as well as with citizens while building awareness and disseminating information, and knowledge of rights and responsibilities. They can and should take a proactive role in bringing together all stakeholders of urban governance and help crystallise among all concerned a tangible common feeling of identity and teamwork.

### Box 7.3

#### *A Civic Cooperation*

Jhunjhunu is the district headquarter town in the Shekhawati region of Rajasthan. As the district is home to many famous business houses including those of Birla, Piramal, Modi, Singhania, Goenka, Poddar and Kanodia, the city is visibly prosperous, benefiting from the generosity of its millionaire residents. Jhunjhunu is also known for its large contribution to the armed forces, many of them martyred, and a tradition of Hindu-Muslim cooperation. But Jhunjhunu really stands out as an example of an engaged citizenry and a responsive civic administration.

With a population of 100,485 (Census 2001), 30 per cent of them Muslims, Jhunjhunu is a Class I city. Its 35 elected ward councillors in turn elect the town mayor. When PRIA and other local groups set up *mohalla samitis* in the town five years ago for garbage collection, little did they know it would evolve into an example for the municipality. Today there is door-to-door free collection of garbage in 12 wards. Responding to the initiative of residents who created parks from garbage dumps, the municipality came out with a scheme where it contributes 70 per cent of the cost of converting empty plots into gardens. The local committees have also worked to create infrastructure such as a marriage hall.

Jhunjhunu's experience says citizen engagement works out best when left to the citizens without any interference from politicians. The case of underground sewerage is an example of that. Despite its size, Jhunjhunu has no underground sewerage system; every resident has septic tanks. An elected woman representative, Sudha Panwar, works to keep her *mohalla* of around 2000 houses clean and her ward also has a *mohalla samiti*. A special problem she faced is of families with their own cows and buffalos generating a lot of animal waste which couldn't be collected by municipal sweeper and was blocking the main drains. Panwar worked out a system of cleaning the drains and hiring tractors to remove the waste before taking it to a garbage dump.

In Jhunjhunu, the work of the local groups has been institutionalised. While this has led to municipal workers not coming as regularly as required, the success of people mobilisation has made up for it. The residents have seen the benefits of local initiatives and continue with them as well as monitoring the work of the local bodies.

*Source:* Sharma (2009).

## Nagara Raj Bill: Experience in Some States

The model Nagara Raj Bill, unveiled by the Ministry of Urban Development as part of the JNNURM, is aimed at creating the same set of three-tier devolutionary governance infrastructure in the urban areas as the Panchayati Raj system in the rural areas. Yet, states have shown remarkable reluctance to replicate the model at their end, especially with respect to participatory democratic governance. Number five of the state-level reforms under JNNURM mandates enactment of Community Participation Law to institutionalise citizen participation and introducing the concept of area *sabha* in urban areas. Based on this, the model Nagara Raj Bill provides for area *sabhas* in part two. This is how it works.

At the base of *Nagara Raj* is the area *sabha*, comprising 1,000 to 1,500 citizens registered in the electoral rolls of their local polling booths. They in turn elect from among themselves an area *sabha* representative (ASR), who would be the member of the local ward committee which in turn comprises ASRs and 10 civil society representatives from citizens' action groups or NGOs. The chair of the ward committee is a member of the local municipality which represents the ward. The ward committees sit under the umbrella of a city's municipal corporation, and the chief municipal officer is permitted to sit in on any of the ward committee meetings at any time.

Some states, notably Rajasthan, Gujarat, Andhra Pradesh and Odisha, have unveiled their versions of the Bill but few except the Rajasthan bill follow the provisions in letter or spirit. The Gujarat draft bill, for instance, has neither provision for area *sabha* nor any scope for community participation or involvement of citizens in municipal functions. The bill provides for a ward committee but restricts their scope to merely advisory functions. Its job is to merely review and aid the corporation and the standing committee and as such, is subject to their control and supervision. No provisions expanding a ward committee to include any representatives of registered voters of the ward exists.

Section 2(g) of the draft bill relies on Section 29A of the Bombay Provincial Municipal Corporations Act which grants complete autonomy to the corporation in determining the constitution of the ward committee and therefore, does not stick to the Section 12 of the model bill which includes "not more than ten persons representing the civil society from the ward, nominated by the municipality.." and "...not less than two-thirds of the members of such Committee shall be the Area Sabha Representatives resident in that ward." That makes it fairly useless for the purpose of community participation.

Even the Odisha draft does not have any provision for area *sabhas*; it provides only for ward committee other than the municipality. The guidelines do not include representation from each area in the ward, only the representation of elector base through nomination by the municipality, which goes against the spirit of community participation. Second, the elected members in the ward committee form a minority with an overwhelming majority, 9 out of 13, being nominated. Even the elected members are from community groups such as RWAs and slum federation and not from the elector base in each electoral part. Third, the meeting of the ward committee is to be conducted annually, and only the chairperson or a majority of members can call additional meetings. Since most of the members are nominated, they are likely to agree with the chairperson. This undermines the spirit of the ward committee as the platform for community participation on a periodic basis. Thus, the guidelines need to incorporate properly the provision for area *sabha* including its footprint mapped to electoral parts.

In Andhra Pradesh, the Ordinance amending the Hyderabad Municipal Corporations Act, 1955 says, "There shall be an Area Sabha Representative for each area. He shall be chosen by the representatives of the Residents Welfare Associations and community based organizations falling within the jurisdiction of the area from among them selves as prescribed [7-A.(2)]." When the area *sabha* members are not the democratically elected representatives of the electorate of an area, there is no community participation. Also, specifying a certain kind of people is not empowerment but may work against it by representing a dominant section of society, yet a minority or special interest groups, such as a traders' collective.

The Maharashtra government passed the Maharashtra Municipal Corporation and Municipal Council (Amendment) Act, 2009 on 13 June 2009 but the proposed bill too was a highly diluted version of the model

Nagara Raj Bill. Many of the provisions on composition, functions, duties, activities and rights of ward committees were not included. The Act provides for area *sabhas* but their members are to be nominated by the municipal corporation. The Act has also clubbed together five polling booth areas, instead of the ideal single one, defeating the very purpose of the bill, which breaks up cities into smaller, more manageable localities with common interests particularly in education, sanitation and security. The Act also denies citizens the right to throw out ineffective functionaries, keeping the power with the commissioner, making it easier for political parties to control the ward committees.

Comments made by a few Mumbai politicians, quoted by the DNA newspaper, indicates why Nagara Raj Bill has a tough battle ahead.[5] "An ASR will represent 1,000 people. Each ward in Borivali has more than 35,000 people which mean 35 people will be elected. We already have 16 councillors so what will the ASRs do?" said Gopal Shetty, BJP Mumbai president. In the same vein, Congress MP Sanjay Nirupam said, "We must make sure that there is no parallel government as a local corporator is also an elected representative." Still, the passing of the Act itself signals a potential for further reforms geared towards increased citizen's participation.

Such an Act would also facilitate participatory budgeting, pioneered by Porto Alegre in Brazil in 1989 and since been replicated in several cities of the world. Recommendations on how and where funds should go could then move from area *sabhas* to the corporation or council to even out in the final budget. In Porto Alegre, for instance, an astonishing number of 50,000, out of a population of 1.5 million, participate in the process that begins in January, moving from the smallest locality to the regions (like wards) to the entire city. Assemblies are held where residents elect 'budget delegates' who in turn identify priorities for budget allocations to vote on them. Such budgeting gave voice to the city's poor living in slums and helped reduce inequalities. For instance, 75 per cent of households had sewage and water connections in 1988 which grew to 98 per cent of households in 1997. In India, by contrast, municipal budgets are made by

---

5.  "Will Nagar Raj Bill Make Mumbaikar the Real King?", *Daily News and Analyisis (DNA)*, Mumbai, 26 May 2009.

bureaucrats, with little or some input by the elected representatives, and passed with minimal debate. The situation is worse in smaller towns as we have seen, where spending of resources benefits few and does not help them grow.

## Politics at the State

The political affiliations do not by and large make a difference in the deliverance of urban governance. In most of the towns surveyed, ward councillors from different parties function together without problems. In Haryana, where money is given for development of the wards, ward councillors belonging to the ruling party at the State Legislature, get preference.

In some towns there is a hint of conflict between parastatal agencies and municipal governments. In Himachal Pradesh, municipal officers, particularly those of progressive towns like Parwanoo, feel that their development plans are jeopardised by the HIMUDA (Himachal Pradesh Housing and Urban Development Authority) which holds on to most of the land and create difficulties. In Haryana, similar problems of parallel functioning are present. In Bihar, government 'line departments' and agencies like agricultural marketing board, fisheries board, etc., pick up revenues from markets whereas the maintenance of the relevant infrastructure remains the responsibility of the municipal government. Town planning is carried out by state government departments, especially those who do not know local conditions and priorities.

## Relationship between Elected Councillors and Executives

Clear conclusions do not emerge here. At most of the municipal offices in the towns surveyed, elected ward councillors and executive staff work in harmony. But exceptions exist. In a *nagar panchayat* called Kanti in Bihar, the relationship between executive and elected wing is so acrimonious that urban governance is seriously affected. This does not necessarily mean that where relations are friendlier, it is a boon for the citizens, because the amicability might be based on collusion over corruption, as perceived in some towns in Bihar and Himachal Pradesh.

## Making ULBs Open, People-friendly and Accountable

Hardly any information related to financial efficiency, service quality or coverage by municipal bodies is shared publicly. By and large, the annual budget is the only formal report prepared by the ULBs. In some states, annual administrative reports and audit reports are also prepared. None of this is disseminated outside. Nor are these reports user-friendly, detailed or standardised. For instance, a figure for capital expenditure on roads may be provided but without any corresponding information on the projects on which this would be incurred. Information on procurement and recruitment is tougher to get.

Even the state government does not have reliable and comparable information on ULBs, which affects their work. For example, any attempt to link discretionary grants to financial performance will fail, since credible information required to assess and compare financial performance is not available.

Naturally, this inhibits attempts by the citizens to understand and help improve ULB performance. Some reforms in areas such as accounting, property tax and e-governance in some municipal bodies have facilitated data gathering and disclosure.[6] Among these is the Municipal Corporation of Hyderabad, which has implemented accrual-based accounting reforms and then initiated an external audit process. Its accounts are now audited by a group of external auditors. As part of its Saukaryam initiative, the Visakhapatnam Municipal Corporation shares procurement information on its website. Similarly, Bruhat Bengaluru Mahanagar Palike has introduced the fund based accounting system and now, with the help of the Public Affairs Centre, conducts public discussions on city finances. Property tax accounts have been made available online by several corporations, after they simplified the property tax assessment system and developed a comprehensive database.

## How Citizens can Test ULBs

The balanced scorecard, which is an effective tool for strategy execution, has been successfully used in the public domain to

---

6. "How Transparent Can Local Bodies Be", *Solutions*, CRISIL Infrastructure Advisory, January 2004.

collaboratively develop and monitor organisational performance measures. Variants of this tool have been used in countries such as the US for measuring the performance of organisations. Use of similar instruments[7] for Indian ULBs can help organisations focus on key social objectives while providing the public and higher levels of government with an accountability mechanism for assessing the performance of a local body. The report card system, pioneered by Bangalore-based Public Affairs Centre, is also useful.

Another way to improve ULB's public/customer interface is by introducing e-governance, which has been successfully used by many state governments to improve the quality of interaction with the citizens as well as the quality of services provided. The Saukaryam initiative of the Visakhapatnam Municipal Corporation and the e-Seva initiative of the government of Andhra Pradesh are instances of e-governance. Karnataka's Bhoomi project is another very good example of e-service for public as well as administrative gains. With the Common Service Centre project gaining ground all over the country, municipal bodies can take advantage of the scheme to put in place an e-governance system to achieve higher collection of taxes as well as improve the quality of life and level of satisfaction for citizens.

---

7.   Joshi and Ray (2005).

# References and Further Reading

3i Network (2006). "Urban Infrastructure", *India Infrastructure Report 2006*. New Delhi: Oxford University Press.

—————. (2008). "Business Models of the Future", *India Infrastructure Report 2008*. New Delhi: Oxford University Press.

—————. (2009). "Land—A Critical Resource for Infrastructure", *India Infrastructure Report 2009*. New Delhi: Oxford University Press.

Bagchi, Soumen (2001). "Financing Capital Investments in Urban Infrastructure—Constraints in Accessing Capital Market by Urban Local Bodies", in *Economic and Political Weekly*, January 27.

Bagchi, Soumen and Anirban Kundu (2003). "Development of Municipal Bond Market in India: Issues Concerning Financing of Urban Infrastructure", *Economic and Political Weekly*, February 22-28.

Bardhan, Pranab (2007). "Political Economy", in Kaushik Basu (ed.), *The Oxford Companion to Economics in India*. OUP.

Basu, Amitava (2001). "Road Map to Municipal Finance Reform", in *Good Urban Governance Campaign-India Launch: Learning from One Another*, UNCHS (HABITAT) and Government of India, New Delhi.

Bird, R. and C. Wallich (1993). "Fiscal Decentralization and Intergovernmental Relations in Transition Economics—Towards a Systemic Framework of Analysis", *Policy Research Working Papers*. Washington DC: The World Bank.

Bird, Richard M., Robert D. Ebel and Christine I. Wallich (1995). *Decentralization of the Socialist State*. Washington DC: The World Bank.

Bird, Richard M. (2000a). "Fiscal Decentralisation and Competitive Governments", in Galeotti, Gianluigi Pierre Salmon and Ronald Wintrobe (eds.), *Competition and Structure: The Political Economy of Collective Decision: Essays in Honor of Albert Breton*. Cambridge University Press.

Bohra, O.P. (1996). *State-Local Fiscal Relations in India*. New Delhi: National Book Shop and Dolphin Publishing House.

Brecht, Bertolt (1939). *To Posterity*. Translated by H.R. Hays.

Chattopadhyay, Soumyadip (2006). "Municipal Bond Market for Financial Urban Infrastructure", in *Economic and Political Weekly*, June 30.

Davis, Mike (2007). *Planet of Slums*. London: Verso Books.

Dhillon, Amrita (2007). "Finance Commission", in Kaushik Basu (ed.), *The Oxford Companion to Economics in India*. OUP.

Government of India (1985). *The Report of the Committee on Octroi*.

————. (1994). *Report of The Tenth Finance Commission*. December.

————. (2000). *Report of The Eleventh Finance Commission*. June.

————. (2004). *Report of The Twelfth Finance Commission*. November.

————. (2008). *The State of Panchayats: 2007-08*. New Delhi: MoPR and Anand: IRMA.

————. (2009). *Economic Survey 2007-08*. Ministry of Finance. pp.250-251.

Government of Rajasthan (2007). "Rural Decentralisation and Participatory Planning for Poverty Reduction", *Rajasthan State Report*. Submitted to the UNDP, New Delhi. March.

IIPA (2005). "Fiscal Decentralization and Finances of Panchayati Raj Institutions in India", *Indian Journal of Public Administration*, New Delhi.

Joshi, Ravikant (2005). "Decentralisation and Local Finance Issues: The Workings of State Finance Commissions in India", ADB's Technical Assistance Project *Policy Research Networking to Strengthen Policy Reforms*. April.

Joshi, Ravikant and Ray, Sanjukta (2005). *Compendium of Urban Performance Indicators*. Mumbai: Youth for Unity and Voluntary Action (YUVA).

Kundu, Amitabh, Soumen Bagchi and Debolina Kundu (1999). "Regional Distribution of Infrastructure and Basic Amenities in Urban India—Issues Concerning Empowerment of Local Bodies", *Economic and Political Weekly* 34(28) July 10.

Kundu, Amitabh (2006). "Trends and Patterns of Urbanization and their Economic Implications", in *India Infrastructure Report 2006*. New Delhi: Oxford University Press.

Mathur, M.P. (1999). "The Constitution (74th) Amendment Act and Urban Local Governments: An Overview", *Urban India* XIX: 1. (Journal of the NIUA), January-June.

Mathur, O.P. (2001). *Approach to State-Municipal Fiscal Relations: Options and Perspectives*. New Delhi: National Institute of Public Finance and Policy.

————. (2006). "Urban Finance", in *India Infrastructure Report 2006*. 3i Network. New Delhi: Oxford University Press.

Mathur, O.P., P. Sengupta and A. Bhaduri (2000). *Option for Closing the Revenue Gap of Municipalities 2000-01 to 2004-05*. New Delhi: NIPFP.

Mathur, O.P. and Sanjukta Ray (2003). *Financing Municipal Services: Reaching Out to Capital Markets*. New Delhi: National Institute of Public Finance and Policy.

Mathur, O.P. and Sandeep Thakur (2004). *India's Municipal Sector, A Study for Twelfth Finance Commission*. New Delhi: National Institute of Public Finance and Policy.

Mishra, C.S. (n.d.). *A Study of the Measures Needed to Augment the Consolidated Fund of the States for Supplementing the Resources of Local Bodies*. Commissioned by the Twelfth Finance Commission.

Mohan, Rakesh (2006). "Asia's Urban Century: Emerging Trends", Key note address delivered at the *Conference of Land and Policies and Urban Development*, Lincoln Institute of Land Policy, Cambridge, Massachusetts, June 5.

Mohanty, P.K., B.M. Misra, Rajan Goyal and P.D. Jeromi (2008). "Muncipal Finance in India: An Assessment, Development Research Group", *Study # 26*, Department of Economic Analysis and Policy, Reserve Bank of India, Mumbai, January.

Musgrave, Richard (1983). "Who should Tax Where and What", in Charles E. Mclure Jr. (ed.), *Tax Assignments in Federal Countries*. Canberra: Australia University Press.

Musgrave, Richard and Peggy Musgrave (1989). *Public Finance in Theory and Practice*. New York: McGraw-Hill.

National Institute of Urban Affairs (1987). *The Nature and Dimensions of the Urban Fiscal Crisis*.

————. (1989). *Revamping the Structure of Property Taxes: A Study*.

————. (1989). *Upgrading Municipal Services: Norms and Financial Implications* (Vols. I & II).

————. (1989). *Resource Mobilisation by Local Bodies in the National Capital Region*.

————. (1990). *Pricing of Urban Services*.

————. (1990). *Municipal Corporation of Delhi: A Study of its Finances*.

————. (1997). "Financing Urban Infrastructure in India", *Research Study Series* No. 59. Prepared for the Urban Sector Profile Project of the Asian Development Bank.

————. (1998a). *A Compendium of Municipal Legislations in Conformity with Constitution (74th) Amendment Act, 1992*. New Delhi: National Institute of Urban Affairs.

————. (1998b). "Abolition of Octroi: A Study of its Impacts on Municipal Finances and Transport Efficiency, for the Ministry of Surface Transport". Government of India.

————. (1996). "Kanpur Municipal Corporation: A Study of its Finances". For the UP State Finance Commission.

————. (1996). "A Study of Municipal Finances for Faridabad and Sonepat". For the Haryana State Finance Commission.

————. (2005). *Impact of the Constitution (74th) Amendment Act, 1992: On the Working of ULBs*. Volume 1. Final Reports. New Delhi: NIUA.

————. (2005). *State Finance Commissions Recommendations and Follow-up Action There on*. Volume I. New Delhi: NIUA.

————. (2006). *Impact Assessment of Training of Women Elected Representatives*. New Delhi: NIUA.

NIUA and NIPFP (1999). "Financial Profile of the Municipalities of Assam, Karnataka, Kerala, Rajasthan and Tamil Nadu". NIUA and NIPFP Study for Eleventh Finance Commission.

OECD (2002). *Revenue Statistics 1965-2001*, Paris.

Oommen, M.A. (2006). "Fiscal Decentralisation to the Sub-State Level Governments", in *Economic and Political Weekly*, March 11.

————. (1998). "Eleventh Finance Commission and Local Bodies: Tasks and Options", *Economic and Political Weekly* XXXIII(51) (19 December).

Rajaraman, Indira and Garima Vasishtha (2000). "Impact of Grants on Tax Effort of Local Government", *Economic and Political Weekly* XXXV(30), August.

Rajaraman, Indira, O.P. Bohra and V.S. Regnanathan (1996). "Augmentation of Panchayati Raj Resources", *Economic and Political Weekly* XXXI(18), May.

Rangarajan, C. (2004). "Issues before the XII Finance Commission", *Economic and Political Weely*: 271, June 26-July 2.

Rao, M. Govinda and Raja J. Chelliah (1991). *Survey of Research on Fiscal Federalism in India*. New Delhi: National Institute of Public Finance and Policy.

Rao, M. Govinda, Tapas Kumar Sen and Pratap R. Jena (2008). "Issues before the Thirteenth Finance Commission", *Working Paper* 2008-55. NIPFP. August.

Rao, M. Govinda (2001). "Fiscal Decentralization in Indian Federalism", *Working Paper* No.98. Bangalore: Institute of Social and Economic Change.

Ray, Sanjukta (2006). "Urban Governance in Small and Medium Towns of India: A Study on Municipal Finance". New Delhi: PRIA.

———. (2007). "Civil Society Voices", Voluntary Action Network India, VANI, September-October 2007. *http://www.vaniindia.org/Download/csv_sep-dec2007.pdf*

Sivaramakrishnan, K.C., Amitabha Kundu and B.N. Singh (2005). *Handbook of Urbanisation in India*. New Delhi: OUP.

Sharma, Kalpana (2009). *India's Small and Medium Towns—A Story of Lost Opportunities*. PRIA, March.

Thakur, Sandeep (2006). "Evaluating the Financial Health of Indian Cities: A Diagnostic Report", *Working Paper* 06-05, December. New Delhi: National Institute of Urban Affairs.

UN-HABITAT, NIUA and the Economic Development Institute of the World Bank (1988). *Urban Management in Asia: Issues and Opportunities*.

UN-HABITAT and World Bank (1990). *Training Manual on Urban Local Government Finance for South Asian Countries: Readings and Case Studies in Urban Finance*. UN-HABITAT and Economic Development Institute, The World Bank.

Vaidya, Chetan and Brad Johnson (2001). "Ahmedabad Municipal Bond: Lessons and Pointers", *Economic and Political Weekly*, July 28.

World Bank (2004). *Fiscal Decentralisation of Rural Governments in India*. Oxford University Press.

# Annexures

**Annexure I**

**Additional Tables**

**Table A-1.1**

*Population of Million-Plus Urban Agglomerations/Cities (2001)*

| Rank | Urban Agglomeration/ City | Population (Million) | Population Growth | | | |
|---|---|---|---|---|---|---|
| | | | 1981-1991 | 1991-2001 | 1981-1991 | 1991-2001 |
| 1. | Greater Mumbai | 16.37 | 33.7 | 29.9 | 20.4 | 20.0 |
| 2. | Kolkata | 13.22 | 19.9 | 19.9 | 6.6 | 4.1 |
| 3. | Delhi | 12.79 | 46.9 | 51.9 | 43.2 | 36.2 |
| 4. | Chennai | 6.42 | 26.4 | 18.5 | 28.9 | 9.7 |
| 5. | Bangalore | 5.69 | 41.3 | 37.8 | 7.4 | 61.3 |
| 6. | Hyderabad | 5.53 | 66.5 | 27.4 | 39.2 | 12.8 |
| 7. | Ahmedabad | 4.52 | 29.5 | 36.4 | 22.9 | 18.9 |
| 8. | Pune | 3.75 | 44.8 | 50.6 | 30.2 | 38.3 |
| 9. | Surat | 2.81 | 64.4 | 85.1 | 62.2 | 62.3 |
| 10. | Kanpur | 2.69 | 23.8 | 32.5 | 25.8 | 35.0 |
| 11. | Jaipur | 2.32 | 49.6 | 53.1 | 49.2 | 59.4 |
| 12. | Lucknow | 2.27 | 65.7 | 35.8 | 70.8 | 36.3 |
| 13. | Nagpur | 2.12 | 36.4 | 27.6 | 33.2 | 26.2 |
| 14. | Patna | 1.71 | 19.7 | 55.3 | 18.1 | 33.4 |
| 15. | Indore | 1.64 | 33.7 | 47.8 | 31.6 | 46.3 |
| 16. | Vadodara | 1.49 | 44.0 | 32.4 | 40.4 | 26.6 |
| 17. | Bhopal | 1.45 | 58.4 | 6.9 | 58.3 | 34.9 |
| 18. | Coimbatore | 1.45 | 19.6 | 31.4 | 15.9 | 13.1 |
| 19. | Ludhiana | 1.40 | 71.8 | 33.7 | 71.7 | 33.7 |
| 20. | Kochi | 1.35 | 38.3 | 18.8 | 13.5 | 2.4 |
| 21. | Visakhapatnam | 1.33 | 75.1 | 25.7 | 33.0 | 28.9 |
| 22. | Agra | 1.32 | 26.9 | 39.4 | 28.5 | 29.2 |
| 23. | Varanasi | 1.21 | 29.3 | 17.5 | 29.6 | 18.4 |
| 24. | Madurai | 1.19 | 19.7 | 10.0 | 14.6 | 1.9 |

*contd...*

*...contd...*

| Rank | Urban Agglomeration/ City | Population (Million) | 1981-1991 | 1991-2001 | 1981-1991 | 1991-2001 |
|------|---------------------------|---------------------|-----------|-----------|-----------|-----------|
| 25.  | Meerut     | 1.17   | 56.5 | 37.4 | 67.9 | 42.5 |
| 26.  | Nashik     | 1.15   | 63.7 | 58.8 | 80.6 | 63.9 |
| 27.  | Jabalpur   | 1.12   | 17.4 | 25.7 | 20.8 | 22.0 |
| 28.  | Jamshedpur | 1.10   | 21.9 | 32.9 | 5.1  | 23.8 |
| 29.  | Asansol    | 1.09   | 52.0 | 42.7 | 42.9 | 85.4 |
| 30.  | Dhanbad    | 1.06   | 18.9 | 30.5 | 26.2 | 31.1 |
| 31.  | Faridabad  | 1.05   | 86.7 | 70.8 | 86.7 | 70.8 |
| 32.  | Allahabad  | 1.05   | 29.9 | 24.3 | 28.7 | 24.9 |
| 33.  | Amritsar   | 1.01   | 19.2 | 42.6 | 19.2 | 27.3 |
| 34.  | Vijayawada | 1.01   | 37.8 | 19.6 | 32.9 | 17.6 |
| 35.  | Rajkot     | 1.00   | 47.1 | 53.1 | 25.7 | 72.8 |
|      | Total      | 107.88 |      |      |      |      |

*Source:* Census of India 1971, 1981, 1991 and 2001.

## Table A-1.2

*List of Identified Cities under JNNURM*

| Serial Number | Name of the City | Name of the State | Population (lakh) |
|---|---|---|---|
| **a) Mega Cities/UAs** | | | |
| 1. | Delhi | Delhi | 128.77 |
| 2. | Greater Mumbai | Maharashtra | 164.34 |
| 3. | Ahmedabad | Gujarat | 45.25 |
| 4. | Bangalore | Karnataka | 57.01 |
| 5. | Chennai | Tamil Nadu | 65.60 |
| 6. | Kolkata | West Bengal | 132.06 |
| 7. | Hyderabad | Andhra Pradesh | 57.42 |
| **b) Million-plus Cities/UAs** | | | |
| 1. | Patna | Bihar | 16.98 |
| 2. | Faridabad | Haryana | 10.56 |
| 3. | Bhopal | Madhya Pradesh | 14.58 |
| 4. | Ludhiana | Punjab | 13.98 |
| 5. | Jaipur | Rajasthan | 23.27 |
| 6. | Lucknow | Uttar Pradesh | 22.46 |
| 7. | Madurai | Tamil Nadu | 12.03 |
| 8. | Nashik | Maharashtra | 11.52 |
| 9. | Pune | Maharashtra | 37.60 |
| 10. | Cochin | Kerala | 13.55 |
| 11. | Varanasi | Uttar Pradesh | 12.04 |
| 12. | Agra | Uttar Pradesh | 13.31 |
| 13. | Amritsar | Punjab | 10.03 |
| 14. | Visakhapatnam | Andhra Pradesh | 13.45 |
| 15. | Vadodara | Gujarat | 14.91 |
| 16. | Surat | Gujarat | 28.11 |
| 17. | Kanpur | Uttar Pradesh | 27.15 |
| 18. | Nagpur | Maharashtra | 21.29 |
| 19. | Coimbatore | Tamil Nadu | 14.61 |
| 20. | Meerut | Uttar Pradesh | 11.61 |
| 21. | Jabalpur | Madhya Pradesh | 10.98 |
| 22. | Jamshedpur | Jharkhand | 11.04 |
| 23. | Asansol | West Bengal | 10.67 |
| 24. | Allahabad | Uttar Pradesh | 10.42 |
| 25. | Vijayawada | Andhra Pradesh | 10.39 |
| 26. | Rajkot | Gujarat | 10.03 |
| 27. | Dhanbad | Jharkhand | 10.65 |
| 28. | Indore | Madhya Pradesh | 16.40 |
| **c) Identified Cities with less than One Million Population** | | | |
| 1. | Guwahati | Assam | 8.19 |
| 2. | Itanagar | Arunachal Pradesh | 0.35 |

*Source: www.jnnurm.nic.in/nurmurdweb/defaultud.aspx*

## Table A-1.3

*Timeline of Progress of First State Finance Commission*

| State | Date of SFC Setup | Report Submitted on | ATR Submitted on | Period to be Covered by SFC |
|---|---|---|---|---|
| Andhra Pradesh | 22.6.1994 | 31.5.1997 | 29.11.1997 | 1997-98 to 1999-2000 |
| Arunachal Pradesh | 21.5.2003 | 6.6.2003 | 3.7.2003 | 2003-04 to 2005-06 |
| Assam | 23.6.1995 | 29.2.1996 | 18.3.1996 | 1996-97 to 2000-01 |
| Bihar | 23.4.1994/2.6.1999* | Not submitted | Not submitted | - |
| Chhattisgarh | 22.8.2003 | Not submitted | - | - |
| Goa | 1.4.1999 | 5.6.1999 | 12.11.2001 | 2000-01 to 2004-05 |
| Gujarat | 15.9.1994 | RLBs–13.7.1998 ULBs-Oct. 1998 | Submitted | 1996-97 to 2000-01 |
| Haryana | 31.5.1994 | 31.3.1997 | 1.9.2000 | 1997-98 to 2000-01 |
| Himachal Pradesh | 23.4.1994 | 30.11.1996 | 5.2.1997 | 1996-97 to 2000-01 |
| Jammu & Kashmir | 24.4.2001 | May 2003 | Not submitted | 2004-05 (Interim) |
| Jharkhand | 28.1.2004 | Not submitted | | Not specified |
| Karnataka | 10.6.1994 | RLBs–5.8.1996 ULBs-30.1.1996 | 31.3.1997 | 1997-98 to 2001-02 |
| Kerala | 23.4.1994 | 29.2.1996 | 13.3.1997 | 1996-97 to 2000-01 |
| Madhya Pradesh | 17.8.1994 | 20.7.1996 | 20.7.1996 | 1996-97 to 2000-01 |
| Maharashtra | 23.4.1994 | 31.1.1997 | 5.3.1999 | 1996-97 to 2000-01 # |
| Manipur | 22.4.1994/31.5.1996 | December 1996 | 28.7.1997 | 1996-97 to 2000-01 |
| Meghalaya | SFC not yet constituted | 73rd Amendment not applicable as traditional local institutions of self-government exist in these states | | |
| Mizoram | SFC not yet constituted | | | |

contd...

...contd...

| State | Date of SFC Setup | Report Submitted on | ATR Submitted on | Period to be Covered by SFC |
| --- | --- | --- | --- | --- |
| Nagaland | SFC not yet constituted | | | |
| Odisha | 21.11.1996/24.8.1998* | 30.12.1998 | 9.7.1999 | 1998-99 to 2004-05 $ |
| Punjab | July 1994 | 31.12.1995 | 13.9.1996 | 1996-97 to 2000-01 |
| Rajasthan | 23.4.1994 | 31.12.1995 | 16.3.1996 | 1995-96 to 1999-2000 |
| Sikkim | 23.4.1997/22.7.1998* | 16.08.1999 | June 2000 | 2000-01 to 2004-05 |
| Tamil Nadu | 23.4.1994 | 29.11.1996 | 28.4.1997 | 1997-98 to 2001-02 |
| Tripura | RLBs-23.4.1994 | RLBs-12.1.1996 | RLBs-01.4.1997 | RLBs-Jan. 1996 to Jan 2001 |
| | ULBs-19.8.1996 | ULBs-17.9.1999 | ULBs-27.11.2000 | ULBs-1999-2000 to 2003-04 |
| Uttar Pradesh | 22.10.1994 | 26.12.1996 | 20.1.1998 | 1996-97 to 2000-01 |
| Uttarakhand | 31.1.2001 | 2002 | 3.7.2004 | 2001-02 to 2005-06 |
| West Bengal | 30.5.1994 | 27.11.1995 | 22.7.1996 | 1996-97 to 2000-01 |

*Note:* *: Date of constitution. In case of Gujarat, the SFC report on RLBs was submitted prior to the reconstitution of the SFC.

#: As per the ATR, the SFC recommendations shall be effective from 1.4.1999.

$: Though SFC was asked to submit the report covering a period of five years from 1.4.1998, its report covers the period from 1998-99 to 2004-05.

*Source:* Report of the Twelfth Finance Commission, Government of India, 2004.

## Table A-1.4

*Timeline of Progress of Second, Third and Fourth State Finance Commissions*

| State | Date of SFC Setup | Report Submitted on | ATR Submitted on | Period to be Covered by SFC |
|---|---|---|---|---|
| Andhra Pradesh | 8.12.1998 | 19.8.2002 | 31.3.2003 | 2000-01 to 2004-05 |
| Arunachal Pradesh | Not constituted | | | |
| Assam | 18.4.2001 | 19.8.2002 | 31.3.2003 | 2000-01 to 2005-06 |
| Bihar | June 1999 | RLB-September 2001 | Not submitted | |
| | | ULE-January 2003 | Not submitted | |
| Chhattisgarh | Not constituted | | | |
| Goa | Not constituted | | | |
| Gujarat | 19.11.2003 | Not submitted | | 2005-06 to 2009-10 |
| Haryana | 6.9.2000 | Not submitted | | 2001-02 to 2005-06 |
| Himachal Pradesh | 25.5.1998 | 24.10.2002 | 24.06.2003 | 2002-03 to 2006-07 |
| Jammu & Kashmir | Not constituted | | | |
| Jharkhand | Not constituted | | | |
| Karnataka | October 2000 | December 2002 | Not submitted | 2003-04 to 2007-08 |
| Kerala | 23.6.1999 | January 2001 | Not submitted | 2000-01 to 2005-06 |
| Madhya Pradesh | 17.6.1999 | July 2003 | Not submitted | 2001-02 to 2005-06 |
| Maharashtra | 22.6.1999 | 30.3.2002 | Not submitted | 2001-02 to 2005-06 |
| Manipur | 03.1.2003 | Submitted | Not submitted | 2001-02 to 2005-06 |
| Meghalaya | | | | |
| Mizoram | | | | |
| Nagaland | | | | |
| Odisha | 5.6.2003 | 25.10.2003 | Not submitted | 2005-06 to 2009-10 |

*contd...*

*...contd...*

| State | Date of SFC Setup | Report Submitted on | ATR Submitted on | Period to be Covered by SFC |
|---|---|---|---|---|
| Punjab | September 2000 | 15.2.2002 | 08.06.2002 | 2001-02 to 2005-06 |
| Rajasthan | 07.05.1999 | 30.08.2001 | 26.03.2002 | 2000-01 to 2004-05 |
| Sikkim | July 2003 | Not submitted | | * |
| Tamil Nadu | 2.12.1999 | 21.5.2001 | 8.5.2002 | 2002-03 to 2006-07 |
| Tripura | 29.10.1999 | 10.4.2003 | Not submitted | 2003-04 to 2007-08 |
| Uttar Pradesh | February 2000 | June 2002 | 30.04.2004 | 2001-02 to 2005-06 |
| Uttarakhand | Not constituted | | | |
| West Bengal | 14.7.2000 | 6.2.2002 | Not submitted | 2001-02 to 2005-06 |
| **Constitution of Third SFC** | | | | |
| Andhra Pradesh | 16.1.2003 Reconstituted on 23.12.2004 | Not submitted | - | 2005-06 to 2009-10 |
| Kerala | 20.9.2004 | Submitted on 23.11.2005 | 16-02-2006 | 2006-07 to 2011-12 |
| Punjab | 20.9.2004 | Not submitted | - | 2006-07 to 2011-12 |
| Tamil Nadu | 14.1.2004 | Not submitted | - | 2007-08 to 2012-13 |
| Himachal Pradesh | 26.5.2005 | Interim report given on 2.11.2007 | - | 2007-08 to 2012-13 |
| Sikkim | 4.3.2009 | Not submitted | - | 2010-11 to 2015-16 |
| Haryana | 31.12.2008 | | | 2006-07 to 2011-12 |
| **Constitution of Fourth SFC** | | | | |
| Kerala | 19.9.2009 | | | One year |
| Tamil Nadu | 3.12.2009 | | | 2012-13 to 2017-18 |

*Note:* * No specific period of coverage has been prescribed.

*Source:* Report of the Twelfth Finance Commission, Government of India, 2004 and various state government websites.

## Table A-1.5

### *Relative Importance of Local Taxes in Selected OECD Countries (2001)*

| Countries | Tax Sources as a Per cent of Total Local Tax Revenues | | | | Local Taxes as a Per cent of GDP | Local Taxes as a Per cent of All Taxes[5] |
| --- | --- | --- | --- | --- | --- | --- |
| | Income[1] | Sales[2] | Property[3] | Other[4] | | |
| **Federal:** | | | | | | |
| Australia | 0.0 | 0.0 | 100.0 | 0.0 | 1.0 | 3.0 |
| Austria | 55.3 | 29.7 | 9.9 | 5.1 | 4.4 | 10.1 |
| Belgium | 86.5 | 13.2 | 0.0 | 0.3 | 2.1 | 4.7 |
| Canada | 0.0 | 1.9 | 91.3 | 6.8 | 2.9 | 8.1 |
| Germany | 78.0 | 6.0 | 15.8 | 0.2 | 2.6 | 7.5 |
| Mexico | 0.0 | 2.6 | 86.7 | 10.8 | 0.1 | 0.8 |
| Switzerland | 84.4 | 0.3 | 15.3 | 0.0 | 5.0 | 14.0 |
| United States | 6.5 | 21.8 | 71.8 | 0.0 | 3.5 | 11.5 |
| **Unweighted Average** | 38.8 | 9.3 | 48.8 | 2.9 | 2.9 | 7.5 |
| **Unitary** | | | | | | |
| Czech Republic | 90.8 | 4.2 | 4.6 | 0.4 | 4.8 | 12.4 |
| Denmark | 93.4 | 0.1 | 6.5 | 0.0 | 15.9 | 32.9 |
| Finland | 95.4 | 0.0 | 4.4 | 0.1 | 9.9 | 21.2 |
| France | 0.0 | 11.5 | 48.2 | 40.4 | 4.4 | 9.7 |
| Greece | 0.0 | 46.3 | 0.0 | 53.8 | 0.4 | 1.0 |
| Hungary | 0.8 | 76.2 | 22.5 | 0.4 | 2.0 | 5.2 |
| Iceland | 78.0 | 7.6 | 14.3 | 0.0 | 8.3 | 22.4 |
| Ireland | 0.0 | 0.0 | 100.0 | 0.0 | 0.6 | 1.8 |
| Italy | 12.2 | 8.6 | 18.6 | 60.6 | 4.8 | 11.4 |
| Japan | 47.4 | 20.7 | 30.9 | 1.0 | 7.0 | 25.6 |
| Korea | 16.6 | 26.5 | 53.3 | 3.6 | 3.9 | 15.1 |
| Luxembourg | 92.9 | 1.3 | 3.8 | 0.3 | 2.4 | 5.9 |
| Netherlands | 0.0 | 44.0 | 56.0 | 0.0 | 1.4 | 3.4 |
| New Zealand | 0.0 | 9.7 | 90.3 | 0.0 | 1.8 | 5.8 |
| Norway | 89.9 | 2.2 | 7.9 | 0.0 | 6.5 | 16.3 |
| Poland | 78.4 | 1.8 | 19.8 | 0.0 | 5.7 | 16.3 |
| Portugal | 21.6 | 33.7 | 44.5 | 0.2 | 2.3 | 6.3 |
| Slovak Republic | 59.9 | 11.8 | 28.2 | 0.1 | 1.5 | 4.0 |
| Spain | 25.2 | 36.1 | 37.3 | 1.4 | 5.9 | 16.9 |
| Sweden | 100.0 | 0.0 | 0.0 | 0.0 | 16.0 | 29.8 |
| Turkey | 24.7 | 31.5 | 6.5 | 37.3 | 4.3 | 13.0 |
| United Kingdom | 0.0 | 0.0 | 99.5 | 0.5 | 1.5 | 4.1 |
| **Unweighted Average** | 38.0 | 16.8 | 31.6 | 9.1 | 4.8 | 12.7 |

*Note:* 1. Includes individual and corporate inocme tax plus payroll tax.

2. Includes general consumption taxes, taxes on goods and services (fuel taxes, hotel and motel occupancy) and taxes on use on goods or on permission to use goods or perform activities.

3. Taxes on property including recurring taxes on net wealth.

4. Includes social security contributions in Austria and some residual taxes mainly on business (Austria, Canada and Germany) and miscellaneous taxes everywhere.

5. Total includes Central government, state government, local government and social security funds.

*Source:* OECD (2002). *Revenue Statistics 1965-2001* (Paris: OECD), Tables 135 to 168.

# Annexure II

## Snapshot of Study Recommendations for Institutions

| State | State Finance Commission | State Government | Municipal Body | Civil Society Organisations |
|---|---|---|---|---|
| Rajasthan | • Recommend some buoyant source of revenue.<br>• Facilitate fiscal transfers and at the same time enforce fiscal responsibility. | • Large scale, all round property tax reforms.<br>• Rationalisation and implementation of user charges for civic services.<br>• Disbursing grants-in-aid in a more transparent, smooth and predictable manner and at the same time imposing fiscal responsibility.<br>• Initiating accounting reforms and giving computer facilities. | • More training to elected and executive staff of the municipal body for all functions, particularly tax collection and accounting and budgeting. | • Enhancing the role of civil society organisations in making democratic decentralisation and people's participation, a reality. |
| Chhattisgarh | • Recommend some buoyant source of revenue.<br>• Facilitate fiscal transfers and at the same time enforce fiscal responsibility. | • Large scale, all round property tax reforms.<br>• Rationalisation and implementation of user charges for civic services.<br>• Disbursing grants-in-aid in a more transparent, smooth and predictable manner, and at the same time imposing fiscal responsibility.<br>• Initiating accounting reforms and giving computer | • Rationalising establishment expenditure and reorienting expenditure priorities away from establishment, towards capital development and operation and maintenance.<br>• Paying adequate attention to all departments of the municipal body, for all round good governance.<br>• The most urgent need is to revamp account keeping, financial reporting | • Enhancing the role of civil society organisations in making democratic decentralisation and people's participation, a reality.<br>• Creating awareness among citizens, and officers about all the nuances of urban governance. |

contd...

*...contd...*

| State | State Finance Commission | State Government | Municipal Body | Civil Society Organisations |
|---|---|---|---|---|
| | | facilities. Imparting training to accounting staff. | and record keeping, and budget preparation. <br> • More training to elected and executive staff of the municipal body for all functions, particularly tax collection. <br> • Own revenue sources of the municipality should be consolidated to allow stable growth, which will enable it to overcome their dependence on revenue grants in the long run. <br> • User charges should be more systematically levied and collected <br> • The municipal officers have to be more competent in planning according to priority (with consultations of all resident stakeholders) and in estimating costs and benefits of developmental works. | |
| Haryana | • SFC should facilitate fiscal transfers and at the same time enforce fiscal responsibility. <br> • Revenue grants for running expenses should be provided to local bodies, but with fiscal responsibility norms. | • All-round tax reforms to enhance municipal own revenue generation are very essential to ensure local autonomy. <br> • Accounting reforms are most urgently called for. <br> • Role of parastatal bodies should be debated and revised, with the objective | • Property taxes are low and should be improved through tax reforms. <br> • Stamp duty is high, but this may not turn out to be a sustainable source of municipal revenue in the long run. So, dependence on it should be controlled and gradually reduced. | • Civil society organisations should be encouraged to provide a platform for citizen's participation and awareness generation regarding the nuances of urban governance. |

*contd...*

*...contd...*

| State | State Finance Commission | State Government | Municipal Body | Civil Society Organisations |
|---|---|---|---|---|
| | | of more autonomy to local governments. | • Grant dependence has been quite high for revenue expenditures but high for capital expenditures. But, unfortunately the full financial potential for developmental works has not been realised. The reasons behind this should be unearthed and the problems (some physical bottlenecks or accounting lapses) should be solved.<br>• Accounts for the receipt and expenditure of capital flows should be much more meticulously and clearly written down and not be restricted to the view of the engineering department. The accounts department should be able to make it fully accessible to the public. Accounts staff need training to use computers effectively.<br>• Sometimes O&M expenditures are being met from funds meant for development. Proper account keeping and other interventions should stop this from happening.<br>• Establishment expenditure is most alarmingly high and the municipalities should give | |

*contd...*

...contd...

| State | State Finance Commission | State Government | Municipal Body | Civil Society Organisations |
|---|---|---|---|---|
| | | | utmost priority to bringing it under control.<br>• The major expenditure, among the various functions of the municipality, is on the salary bill of the solid waste management and sanitation department and capital expenditure in the public works department. The rest of the functions suffer neglect. This should be reviewed and spending priorities should be more balanced.<br>• There should be a more holistic development of the city by paying more attention to other departments too, such as Health, Environment, Planning and Regulation. More capital grants should be earmarked for these neglected departments.<br>**Parwanoo** | |
| Himachal Pradesh | • They should recommend buoyant source of revenue like octroi.<br>• Recommend enough financial transfers to cover running expenses.<br>• Recommend specific purpose capital grants for functions that are neglected.<br>• Impose fiscal responsibility norms. | • Enable appropriate property tax reforms.<br>• Revise rates of user charges.<br>• Continue to give financial transfers at the same time imposing fiscal responsibility.<br>• Revise role of parastatal bodies (HIMUDA).<br>• Disburse capital grants | • The MC should sustain its efficient collection of tax and non-tax revenues.<br>• If money is being wasted on maintaining infrastructure, capital investment should be made to replace it.<br>• With good tax collection record, it may explore the option of taking loans for infrastructure development. | • Create awareness among citizens about various aspects of urban governance, especially about dumping garbage, and the necessity to pay tax.<br>• To encourage direct citizen's participation by providing a platform for information sharing. |

contd...

*...contd...*

| State | State Finance Commission | State Government | Municipal Body | Civil Society Organisations |
|---|---|---|---|---|
| | • Review the role of parastatal bodies. | smoothly and transparently.<br>• Enable accounting reforms and improve its own records of municipal finances (record financial flows in greater detail and avoid use of consolidated heads, record liabilities separately, don't list security deposits with other income sources). | • Keep better accounts of capital grants.<br>• Pay more heed to citizen's wishes/priorities, in carrying out developmental works. Accounts should be more detailed<br>**Nagrota Bagwan**<br>• Tax collection should be improved, non-tax revenue collection should be sustained at the present high level, establishment expenditures should be controlled, accounts should be kept in more detail.<br>**Bilaspur**<br>• Tax collection needs to be improved, property tax should be levied.<br>**Dharamshala**<br>• Establishment expenditures should be kept in check.<br>• Should address poor service delivery in spite of relatively better financial health.<br>• Executive and elected officers should be more responsive and sensitive to citizens and strive to make urban governance more inclusive. | |

*contd...*

| State | State Finance Commission | State Government | Municipal Body | Civil Society Organisations |
| --- | --- | --- | --- | --- |
| Madhya Pradesh | • They should recommend buoyant source of revenue like octroi.<br>• Recommend enough financial transfers to cover running expenses.<br>• Recommend specific purpose capital grants for functions that are neglected.<br>• Impose fiscal responsibility norms.<br>• Review the role of parastatal bodies. | • It should make all round efforts to undertake tax reforms by revising the tax rates. They should initiate accounting and budgetary reforms with a focus to rationalise and simplify accounting and budget structure. | **Manali**<br>• Given its good revenue collection, it should tap the capital market to raise loans for capital development. Its establishment expenditure should be checked. Accounts should be kept in more detail.<br>• The municipality must consolidate its efforts to generate more revenue from its own sources, namely taxes, fees, fines and user charges.<br>• Property tax collections should improve, through appropriate tax reforms.<br>• Accounting systems, financial record keeping and budgeting processes need urgent improvement. There is much detail in some items, but recorded in a convoluted and confusing manner. Yet for some items, only totals have been put down for widely varying components. More rationality, logic and systematic classification are needed in the entire financial record keeping, accounting and budget document writing processes.<br>• User charges must be consolidated and their collection should be more regular and sustained. | • Platforms should be built by civil society groups to nurture citizen's participation. The ward committee should be a good starting point. |

contd...

...contd...

| State | State Finance Commission | State Government | Municipal Body | Civil Society Organisations |
|---|---|---|---|---|
| | | | • Expenditure on establishment is moderately high, but its growth should be checked.<br>• Capital development expenditure should be undertaken since the financial capacity exists. Bottlenecks in this regard should be identified and confronted. Better accounts have to be kept of capital flows (receipts and expenditures).<br>• Expenditures should not be so totally skewed in favour of public works only. This is not conducive to the balanced development of the city. | |
| Bihar | • Income from wholesale agricultural markets should be restored to the ULBs.<br>• Must ensure that ULBs get a fair share of advertisement tax, toll tax, entertainment tax and service tax (some of these devolutions are now going to the parastatals).<br>• Should ensure that ULBs continue to receive generous transfers from the state government until their own revenue collection recovers. | • Must give the ULBs at least some land to enable them to perform basic service delivery (e.g., landfill site for solid waste management).<br>• Should promptly disburse state and Central government grants for urban development and services to municipal governments, instead of lower level district administration.<br>• Must impart training to newly elected representatives, who have been voted to power after local government elections ordained by the 74th Amendment.<br>• Must make sure that property tax reforms initiated at Patna | • Must try to compile and maintain data on financial flows from ledger books, in a logical format.<br>• Must begin the budget preparation process.<br>• Tax department must be strengthened.<br>• Proceeds of municipal tax collection must be entered in the accounts before spending them directly. (This present practice, apart from being very unsound financially, leads to the problematic case of 'temporary embezzlement').<br>• Rates of fees, fines, charges, must be revised. Rents on | Civil society organisations should be encouraged to provide a platform for citizen's participation and awareness generation regarding the nuances of urban governance. |

contd...

*...contd...*

| State | State Finance Commission | State Government | Municipal Body | Civil Society Organisations |
|---|---|---|---|---|
| | • Must ensure that the state government awards either revenue sources or financial transfer for ULBs to bear establishment and O&M costs.<br>• Must conduct research into the age–old dragnet of control and autocracy of the state government, which effectively stops ULBs from exercising all the rights granted to them by the 74th Amendment.<br>• Municipalities can, without the permission of the state government, spend no more than Rs. 10,000 (by Section 68, Bihar and Odisha Municipal Act, 1922). This outdated limit must be revised.<br>• Must enforce a time limit for the state government to respond to the application of ULBs to revise tax rates.<br>• Recommend a separate cadre for municipal staff and formation of an effective urban directorate. | are replicated in all towns. | municipal property should be periodically and appropriately revised.<br>• Good accounting practices should be initiated on a war footing.<br>• Must make sure that funds for developmental works and for running expenses are not mixed up and used interchangeably at will. Good accounting practices, enabled by state government would correct much of this problem. | |

# Annexure IIIa

*Sample Page of PRIA Municipal Budget Handbook in Hindi
for Citizens in Chhattisgarh*

## अपने निकाय के बजट के भाग

किसी भी स्थानीय निकाय के बजट को दो भागों राजस्व खाते, एवं पूँजी खाते में विभाजित किया जा सकता है परन्तु लेखे की सुविधा के आधार पर स्थानीय निकाय के बजट के कुल 2 भाग होते हैं: (1) आय (2) व्यय

## आय के प्रमुख शीर्ष

- कर
- विशेष अधिनियम
- राजस्व
- अनुदान
- जलकर
- विविध
- असाधारण एवं ऋण

## व्यय के प्रमुख शीर्ष

- प्रशासन एवं संग्रहण
- सार्वजनिक सुरक्षा
- जनस्वास्थ्य एवं सुविधायें
- लोक निर्माण
- सार्वजनिक शिक्षा
- विविध
- असाधारण एवं ऋण

## अपने निकाय के बजट में आय एवं व्यय (उदाहरणार्थ)

| आय | | व्यय | |
|---|---|---|---|
| मद | रू. (लाख में) | मद | रू. (लाख में) |
| नगर पालिका कर | 70.78 | प्रशासन एवं संग्रहण | 23.84 |
| विशेष अधिकार | 00.02 | सार्वजनिक सुरक्षा | 29.50 |
| राजस्व अधिनियम | 21.40 | जन स्वास्थ्य | 167.29 |
| अनुदान | 131.00 | लोक निर्माण | 101.00 |
| जलदान | 9.70 | सार्वजनिक शिक्षा | 30.74 |
| विविध | 8.40 | विविध | 14.75 |
| असाधारण ऋण | 43.70 | असाधारण ऋण | 13.12 |

विभिन्न आय शीर्ष के अन्तर्गत आनेवाली मदें

(1)  नगर पालिका/पंचायत कर

    (अ)  क्रय भूमि पर कर

    (ब)  वाहनों और पशुओं पर कर

    (स)  पशुकर

### Annexure IIIb

*PRIA Document for Circulation in Jhunjhunu for Better*
*Municipal Governance Practices*

# Find Out How Your Municipal Council Is Functioning

## Do You Know What Your Municipal Council is Supposed To Do For You and Your Town?

1. Ensure health and hygiene—this includes cleaning of streets, sewers, removing filth and rubbish and provide public vaccination.

2. Enforce some rules for your all round protection—regulating offensive trades (like household industries using harmful chemicals, for example, leather works, stonework, jewellery etc.), removing dangerous buildings, obstructions and projections on streets, regulating burial grounds, disposal of dead animals, stray animals, cattle etc.

3. Provide fire protection, streetlights, develop public streets, public conveniences, markets, drains, sewers, tanks, wells etc.

4. Provide for birth and death registration and promote family welfare.

## Do You Know What More Your Municipal Council Can Be Expected To Do?

1. Develop and maintain parks and gardens, libraries, museums, asylums, halls and other public places.

2. Undertake social welfare measures like housing for the poor, promotion of public health and infant welfare, contributing to public welfare funds, establishing labour welfare centres etc.

3. Taking a census and encouraging vital statistics coverage.

4. Maintain sewage on private premises, set-ups for sewage disposal.

5. Entertainment and recreation.

6. Organise public functions, setting up shops and stalls, holding fairs and exhibitions, supply of milk.

7. Establish and maintain hospitals and dispensaries, maternity centres and child clinics, maintenance of ambulance service, establishing primary schools and orphanages etc.

8. Some other functions, like planning for economic and social development, promotion of public health, safety, education and economic condition of the masses.

The Municipal Council needs money to perform all these duties. They are not being able to perform these duties to your satisfaction, because the money that they collect from the citizens of the town is not enough.

## Do You Know Where They Get the Money From?

Like all governments, their money also comes from you—the citizen. No government has money of its own.

## Do You Know, in What Forms Your Municipal Council Collects Money? In Other Words, What are its Sources of Income?

1. *Tax*

- Property tax

2. *Non-Tax*

- Rent from shops, • Building sanction fees, • Fees for duplicate copies, • Hoarding fees, • Birth and death registration fees, • *Rickshaw* and *thela* fees, • Interest on investments, • Application fees, • Fees for bylaws, • Road cutting charges, • Profit on sale of assets, • Sale of skin of dead animals, • Income from sale of skeleton, • Income from dispensary, • Premium on lease of land, • License for food selling units, • Fees from slaughterhouse, • Tender for fisheries, • Preparation of forms and other documents relating to bylaws

3. *Money given by state government to meet running expenses (wages and salaries, office expenses, maintaining and daily running of civic services)*

   - Compensation to your municipality for abolishing octroi tax (Municipalities used to levy this tax on commercial vehicles entering the town. It has been abolished and the state government gives compensation to the municipalities)

4. *Money from sale of assets (e.g., land buildings etc.)*

5. *Money from Central and state governments for specified development work (to build something new)*

### Where Does Your Municipal Council Spend Money?

The Municipal Council has to spend money on:

* Paying salaries to its employees;

* Running its offices;

* Doing its day to day duties (for example, street sweeping, maintaining streetlights, collecting and disposing garbage);

* Building new constructions or buying new things for the betterment of the town (for example, roads, sewer lines, streetlights, garbage bins or garbage transporting vehicles).

### Do You Know that the Money it Gets from the Citizens of the Town is Much Less Than What it Needs?

* The tax and non-tax income that come to the Municipal Council from you (citizens) is only Rs. 62.43 per person per year for all the duties that it is expected to perform to your town.

* It spends about Rs. 300 per person per year to meet its running expenses (salary payments, office expenses, and day to day services) and about Rs. 150 per person per year for building new constructions for the town.

### Then, how does it Manage the Gap between Income and Expenses?

The state government and the Central government give the money. Your Municipal Council performs its duties to you with 80 per cent money given to it by the state and Central governments and only 20 per cent money it receives from you. The money that the state and Central governments give to the Municipal Council is also your money, paid in the form of various taxes. It is a pool of all the citizens' money across the whole state or country, and you have very little control over it. It is very unlikely that the higher governments would be able to fulfil all the local needs. The money you directly pay to the Municipal Council is directly used to serve you and through your local ward councillor, you have much greater control over it.

### Would you be Happy With This Situation of Your Municipal Council, which is the Closest Government to You?

• If your Municipal Council depends on the state government to this extent, then the control of state government over resources will increase and conversely the control of Municipal Council will decrease. With greater control over your town, state government will take decisions on providing services to you instead of your own Municipal Council.

- The Municipal Council is closer to you, understands the nature of your town and knows your needs better than the state government which is far away.

- You can reach your Municipal Council more easily, than the state government in your state capital.

- You can ask questions to your own ward councillor more easily than the other elected representatives.

- In a local crisis, your Municipal Council can be at your side much faster and more meaningfully than a government, which is far away.

- At present it is difficult for your Municipal Council to perform any of these roles having very little financial support from you, therefore, having to depend heavily on whatever money the state and Central governments give to them.

- Your own Municipal Council can perform all these roles provided it strengthens the financial health based on income from its own citizens.

## Do not You Want to Strengthen Your Own Municipal Council? Know More about the Problems?

- Your Municipal Council spends Rs. 215 per person per year on running expenses. The largest amount of it goes to pay the salaries of the Municipal Council employees, which is about Rs. 150 per person per year. A smaller amount is spent on day-to-day service delivery, which is about Rs. 55 per person per year.

- You may find out the number of employees in the municipality for various jobs. You may need sufficient number of health workers or sweepers to provide such services, however, you may not like redundant clerical staff in the municipality. It's your right to expect that the Municipal Council controls the growth of salary bill.

- You may want to see a higher percentage of spending on the civic service delivery system.

- Among all the departments of the Municipal Council, the public works department spends most of the money (Rs. 110.49 per person per year, 56 per cent), followed by the health department (Rs. 109.72 per person per year, 30 per cent). So, these two departments get most attention from the Municipal Council in terms of spending which leaves very little resources for (14 per cent) all other functions like planning (Re. 0.47 per person per year), solid waste management and sanitation (Rs. 23 per person per year), civic amenities (nil), environment (Rs. 4.57 per person per year), poverty alleviation and social welfare, etc.

## Would You Not Want the Council to Pay Attention to All These Departments? Otherwise, in the Long Run Your Town Will Be Dirty, Poverty-ridden, Unplanned, Environmentally Polluted and Lack Civic Amenities

- The accounts of your municipality are not properly written and financial records are not in order. The records maintained are unnecessarily complex and difficult to understand. So, it is also difficult to ask appropriate questions. As you know, this always leads to wastage of resources and fosters corruption. Even ward councillors many a time do not know about finances of the municipality.

- Tax rates charged to the citizens are very low and outdated, yet there is very high tax evasion.

- Many citizens do not want to pay for basic services, because they are not satisfied with them.

- So, your Municipal Council is not performing its duties to you mainly because it does not have enough money, and partly because of some genuine difficulties.

## Your Municipal Council Needs Your Help and Involvement. Will You Come Forward and Help it to Serve You Better?

This is what you can do on your own:

- Pay your taxes and user charges regularly, honestly and willingly, and make your neighbours do the same.

- Everybody uses basic services, and everyone is already spending money to pay for them, either to government, or to private vendors (whose quality of product is out of your control). When services are not enough, you face problems that make you spend money (getting medical treatment for diseases caused by dirty water or unclean environment, or getting your vehicle repaired because of bad road conditions, or spending more on petrol because public transport system is not good enough, sending your children to expensive private schools because municipal schools are not good enough).

- You may not have to spend all this money if each of you pay your taxes, fees and charges regularly. The Municipal Council will be able to provide basic civic services, giving you a smoother running city with a clean, disease-free environment, and you can hold them accountable through your ward councillor.

- Your city is your child. Your well-being and your future generation's health and security depend on it. Your city government has no magic lamp to generate money. Won't you stand by it and help it to serve you better? You can do so by paying your taxes and fees.

## What Else You Can Do, With Help from the Ward Councillors and Social Workers?

- Individually, or in a group, meet your ward councillor for discussion. If s/he does not cooperate, remind him/her that it's your right as a voter.

- Tell the councillor on what items you want your municipality to spend money, given the present state of services and what you feel as your most urgent need.

- Give your suggestions on how they can get more money.

- Keep a tab on their income and spending. Create pressure on the Municipal Council to write its accounts properly, in a way that all citizens can clearly understand. This is possible.

- Everybody keeps accounts of daily earnings and expenses. The government's accounts are basically the same. If you see any irregularity, raise your concern.

- Ask about the staffing pattern. Create pressure for more staff that directly serve citizens' needs, and less on redundant administrative/bureaucratic/clerical staff.

The basic services of your city depend on your belonging, your involvement and your support.

*Note:*   The figures mentioned here are as per actual expenses for the year 2003-04.

## Annexure IV

*Constitution (74th Amendment) Act, 1992*

# Part IX A

## The Municipalities

243P   In this part, unless the context otherwise requires,

(a)  "Committee" means a Committee constituted under Article 243S;

(b)  "district" means a district in a State;

(c)  "Metropolitan area" means an area having a population of ten lakhs or more, comprised in one or more districts and consisting of two or more Municipalities or Panchayats or other contiguous areas, specified by the Governor by Public notification to be a metropolitan area for the purposes of this Part;

(d)  "Municipal area" means the territorial area of a Municipality as is notified by the Governor;

(e)  "Municipality" means an institution of Self-Government constituted under Article 243Q;

(f)  "Panchayat" means a Panchayat constituted under Article 243B;

(g)  "population" means the Population as ascertained at the last preceding census of which the relevant figures have been published.

243Q   (1)  There shall be constituted in every State,

(a)  a Nagar Panchayat (by whatever name called) for a transitional area, that is to say, an area in transition from a rural area to an urban area;

(b)  a Municipal Council for a smaller urban area; and

(c)  a Municipal Corporation for a larger urban area, in accordance with the provisions of this Part:

Provided that a Municipality under this clause may not be constituted in such urban area or part thereof as the Governor may, having regard to the size of the area and the Municipal services being provided or proposed to be provided by an industrial establishment in that area and such other factors as he may deemed fit, by public notification, specify to be an industrial township.

(2) In this article, "a transitional area", "a smaller urban area" or "a larger urban area" means such area as the Governor may, having regard to the population of the area, the density of the population therein, the revenue generated for local administration, the percentage of employment in non-agricultural activities, the economic importance or such other factors as he may deem fit, specify by public notification for the purposes of this Part.

243R (1) Save as provided in clause (2),

all the seats in a Municipality shall be filled by persons chosen by direct election from the territorial constituencies in the Municipal area and for this purpose each Municipal area shall be divided into territorial constituencies to be known as wards.

(2) The legislature of a State, may, by law, provide:

(a) for the representation in a Municipality of:

(i) persons having special knowledge or experience in local administration;

(ii) the members of the House of the People and the members of the Legislative Assembly of the State representing constituencies which comprise wholly or partly the Municipal area;

(iii) the members of the Council of States and the members of the Legislative Council of the State registered as electors within the Municipal area;

(iv) the Chairpersons of the Committees constituted under clause (5) of article 243S:

Provided that the persons referred to paragraph, (i) shall not have the right to vote in the meetings of the Municipality;

(b) the manner of election of the chairperson of a Municipality.

243S (1) There shall be constituted Wards Committees, consisting or one or more wards, within the territorial area of a Municipality having a population of three lakhs or more.

(2) The legislature of a State, may, by law, make provision with respect to:

(a) The composition and the territorial area of a Wards Committee;

(b) The manner in which the seats in a Wards Committee shall be filled.

(3) A member of a Municipality representing a ward within the territorial area of the Wards Committee shall be a member of that committee.

(4) Where a Wards Committee consists of:

(a) one ward, the member representing that ward in the Municipality; or

(b) two or more wards, one of the members representing such wards in the Municipality elected by the members of the Wards Committee, shall be the Chairperson of that Committee.

(5) Nothing in this article shall be deemed to prevent the Legislature of a State from making any provision for the constitution of Committees in addition to the Wards Committees.

243T (1) Seats shall be reserved for the Scheduled Castes and the Scheduled Tribes in every Municipality and the number of seats so reserved shall bear, as nearly as may be, the same proportion to the total number of sets to be filled by direct election in that Municipality as the population of the Scheduled Castes in the Municipal area or of the Scheduled Tribes in the Municipal area bears to the total population of that area and such seats may be allotted by rotation to different constituencies in a Municipality.

(2) Not less than one-third of the total number of seats reserved under clause (1) shall be reserved for women belonging to the Scheduled Castes or, as the case may be, the Scheduled Tribes.

(3) Not less than one-third (including the number of seats) reserved for women belonging to the Scheduled Castes and the Scheduled Tribes) of the total number of seats to be filled by direct election in every Municipality shall be reserved for women and such seats may be allotted by rotation to different constituencies in a Municipality.

(4) The officers of chairpersons in the Municipalities shall be reserved for the Scheduled Castes, the Scheduled Tribes and women in such manner as the legislature of a State, may by law, provide.

(5) The reservation of seats under clauses (1) and (2) and the reservation of officers of chairpersons (other than the reservation for women) under clause (4) shall cease to have effect on the expiration of the period specified in article 334.

(6) Nothing in this Part, shall prevent the Legislature of a State from making any provision for reservation of seats in any Municipality or offices of Chairpersons in the Municipalities in favour of backward class of citizens.

243U  (1)  Every Municipality unless sooner dissolved under any law for the time being in force, shall continue for five years from the date appointed for its first meeting and no longer:

Provided that a Municipality shall be given a reasonable opportunity of being heard before its dissolution.

(2)  No amendment of any law for the time being in force shall have the effect of causing dissolution of a Municipality at any level, which is functioning immediately before such amendment, till the expiration of its duration specified in clause (1).

(3)  An election to constitute a Municipality shall be completed:

(a)  before the expiry of its duration specified in clause (1);

(b)  before the expiration of a period of six months from the date of its dissolution:

Provided that where the reminder of the period for which the dissolved Municipality would have continued is less than six months, it shall not be necessary to hold any election under this clause for constituting the Municipality for such period.

(4)  A Municipality constituted upon the dissolution of a Municipality before the expiration of its duration shall continue only for the reminder of the period for which the dissolved Municipality would have continued under clause (1) had it not been so dissolved.

243V  (1)  A person shall be disqualified for being chosen as, and for being, a member of a Municipality:

(a)  if he is so disqualified by or under any law for the time being in force for the purposes of elections to the Legislature of the State concerned:

Provided that no person shall be disqualified on the ground that he is less than twenty-five years of age, if he has attained the age of twenty-one years;

(b)  if he so disqualified by or under any law made by the Legislature of the State.

(2)  If any question arises as to whether a member of a Municipality has become subject to any of the disqualifications mentioned in clause (1), the question shall be referred for the decision of such authority and in such manner as the Legislature of a State may, by law, provide.

243W   (1) Subject to the provisions of this Constitution, the Legislature of the State may, by law, endow:

(a)   the Municipalities with such powers and authority as may be necessary to enable them to function as institutions of Self-Government and such law may contain provisions for the devolution of powers and responsibilities of Municipalities, subject to such conditions as may be specified therein, with respect to:

(i)   the preparation of plans for economic development and social justice;

(ii)   the performance of functions and the implementation of schemes as may be entrusted to them including those in relation to the matters listed in the Twelfth Schedule;

(b)   the Committees with such power and authority as may be necessary to enable them to carry out the responsibilities conferred upon them including those in relation to the matters listed in the Twelfth Schedule.

243X   The Legislature of a State may, by law,

(a)   authorise a Municipality to levy, collect and appropriate such taxes, duties, tolls and fees in accordance with such procedure and subject to such limits;

(b)   assign to a Municipality such taxes, duties, tolls and fees levied and collected by the State Government for such purposes and subject to such conditions and limits;

(c)   provide for making such grants in aid to the Municipalities from the Consolidated Fund of the State; and

(d)   provide for constitution of such Funds for crediting all moneys received, respectively, by or on behalf of the Municipalities and also for the withdrawal of such money therefrom, as may be specified in the law.

243Y   (1) The Finance Commission constituted under article 243-I shall also review the financial position of the Municipalities and make recommendations to the Governor as to:

(a)   the principles, which should govern:

(i)   The distribution between the State and the Municipalities of the net proceeds of the taxes, duties, tolls and fees leviable by the State, which may be divided between them under this Part and the allocation between the Municipalities at all levels of their respective shares of such proceeds;

(ii) The determination of the taxes, duties, tolls and fees, which may be assigned to or appropriated by the Municipalities;

(iii) The grants in aid to the Municipalities from the consolidated fund of the State;

(b) the measures needed to improve the financial position of the Municipalities;

(c) any other matter referred to the Finance Commission by the Governor in the interests of sound finance of the Municipalities.

(2) The Governor shall pass every recommendation made by the Commission under this article together with an explanatory memorandum as to the action taken thereon to be laid before the Legislature of the State.

243Z The Legislature of a State may, by law, make provisions with respect to the maintenance of accounts by the Municipalities and the auditing of such accounts.

243ZA (1) electoral rolls for and the conduct of all election to the Municipalities shall be vested in the State Election Commission referred to in article) The Superintendence, direction and control of the preparation of 243K.

(2) Subject to the provisions of this Constitution the Legislature of a State may, by law, make provision with respect to all matters relating to, or in connection with, elections to the Municipalities.

243ZB The provisions of this Part shall apply to the Union Territories and shall, in their application to a Union Territory, have effect as if the references to the Governor of a State were references to the Administrator of the Union Territory appointed under Article 239 and references to the Legislature or the Legislative Assembly of a State were references in relation to a Union Territory having Legislative Assembly, to that Legislative Assembly:

Provided that the President may, by public notification, direct that the provisions of this Part, shall apply to any Union Territory or part thereof subject to such exceptions and modifications as he may specify in the Notification.

243ZC (1) Nothing in this Part shall apply to the Scheduled Areas referred to in clause (1), and the tribal areas referred to in clause (2), of Article 244.

(2) Nothing in this Part shall be construed to affect the functions and the powers of the Darjeeling Gorkha hill Council constituted under any law for the time being in force for the Hill areas of the District of Darjeeling in the State of West Bengal.

(3) Notwithstanding anything in this Constitution, Parliament may, by law, extend the provisions of this Part to the Scheduled Areas and the tribal areas referred to in Clause (1) subject to such exceptions and modifications as may be specified in such law, and no such law shall be deemed to be an amendment of this Constitution for the purposes of Article 368.

243ZD (1) There shall be constituted in every State at the district level a District Planning Committee to consolidate the plans prepared by the Panchayats and the Municipalities in the district and to prepare a draft development plan for the District as a whole.

(2) The Legislature of a State may, by law, make provision with respect to—

(a) the composition of the District Planning Committees;

(b) the manner in which the seats in such Committee shall be filled:

Provided that not less than four-fifths of the total number of members of such Committee shall be elected by, and from amongst, the elected members of the Panchayats at the district level and of the Municipalities in the district in proportion to the ratio between the population of the rural areas and of the urban areas in the district;

(c) the functions relating to district planning which may be assigned to such Committees;

(d) the manner in which the Chairpersons of such committees shall be chosen.

(3) Every District Planning committee shall, in preparing the draft development plan,

(a) have regard to—

(i) matters of common interest between the Panchayats and the Municipalities including spatial planning, sharing of water and other physical and natural resources, the integrated development of infrastructure and environmental conservation;

(ii) the extent and type of available resources whether financial or otherwise;

(b) consult such institutions and organisations as the Governor may, by order, specify.

(4) The Chairperson of every District Planning Committee shall forward the development plan, as recommended by such Committee to the Government of the State.

243ZE (1) there shall be constituted in every Metropolitan area a Metropolitan Planning Committee to prepare a draft development plan for the Metropolitan area as a whole.

(2) The Legislature of a State may, by law, make provisions with respect to:

(a) the composition of the Metropolitan Planning Committees;

(b) the manner in which the seats in such Committees shall be filled:

Provided that not less than two-thirds of the members of such committee shall be elected by, and from amongst the elected members of the Municipalities and Chairpersons of the Panchayats in the Metropolitan area in proportion to the ratio between the population of the Municipalities and of the Panchayats in that area;

(c) the representations in such Committees of the Government of India and the Government of the State and of such organisations and institutions as may be deemed necessary for carrying out the functions assigned to such committees;

(d) the functions relating to planning and co-ordination for the Metropolitan area which may be assigned to such Committees;

(e) the manner in which the chairpersons of such committees shall be chosen.

(3) Every Metropolitan Planning Committee shall, in preparing the draft development plan,

(a) have regard to:

(i) the plans prepared by the Municipalities and the Panchayats in the Metropolitan Area;

(ii) matters of common interest between the Municipalities and the Panchayats, including coordinated spatial planning of the area, sharing of water and other physical and natural resources, the integrated development of infrastructure and environmental conservation;

(iii) the overall objectives and priorities set by the Government of India and the Government of the State;

(iv) the extent and nature of investments likely to be made in the Metropolitan area by agencies of the Government of India and of the Government of the State and other available resources whether financial or otherwise;

(b) consult such institutions and organisations as the Governor may, by order, specify.

(4) The Chairperson of every Metropolitan Planning Committee shall forward the development plan, as recommended by such committee, to the Government of the State.

243ZF Notwithstanding anything in this Part, any provision of any law relating to Municipalities in force in a State immediately before the commencement of the Constitution (Seventy-fourth Amendment) Act, 1992, which is inconsistent with the provisions of this Part, shall continued to be in force until amended or repealed by a competent Legislature or other competent authority or until the expiration of one year from such commencement, whichever is earlier:

Provided that all the Municipalities existing immediately before such commencement shall continue till the expiration of their duration, unless sooner dissolved by a resolution passed to that effect by the Legislative Assembly of that State, or, in case of a State having a Legislative Council, by each House of the Legislature of that State.

243ZG Notwithstanding anything in this Constitution,

(a) the validity of any law relating to the delimitation of constituencies or the allotment of seats to such constituencies, made or purporting to be made under article 243ZA shall not be called I question in any Court;

(b) no election to any Municipality shall be called I question except by an election petition presented to such authority and in such manner as is provided for by or under any law made by the Legislature of A State.

# Annexure V

*Structure of Sub-national Governments in Major Democracies*

| Country | Intermediate | Local |
| --- | --- | --- |
| **Industrial Countries** | | |
| Canada | 10 provinces, 2 territories | 4,507 municipalities |
| France | 22 regions, 96 departments | 36,772 communes |
| Germany | 13 states, 3 city-states | 329 counties, 115 county-free cities, 14,915 municipalities |
| Italy | 22 regions, 93 provinces | 8,100 municipalities |
| Japan | 47 prefectures | 655 cities, 2,586 towns |
| Spain | 17 autonomous communities | 50 provinces, 8,907 municipalities |
| United Kingdom | Counties | 540 rural districts, metropolitan districts, and London boroughs . |
| United States | 50 States, F.D. | 39,000 counties and municipalities, 44,000 special-purpose local authorities |
| **Other Countries** | | |
| Argentina | 23 provinces | 1,617 *municipios* |
| Bangladesh | Not applicable | 4 city corporations, 129 *pourashabha* (smaller municipalities), 4500 Union *parishad* (which group 85,500 villages) |
| Brazil | 27 states, F.D. | 4,974 *municipios* |
| Colombia | 32 departments, F.D. | 1,068 municipalities |
| Ethiopia | 9 regions, plus 2 special city administration, 66 zones | 550 *woredas* |
| India | 28 states, 7 Union territories | 3,586 urban local bodies (95 municipal corporations, 1,436 municipal councils, 2,055 *nagar panchayats*), 234,078 rural local bodies |
| Iran | 25 provinces | 720 districts and municipalities |
| Kenya | 39 county councils | 52 municipal, town and urban councils |
| Korea | 6 special cities, 9 provinces | 67 cities, 137 counties |
| Malaysia | 13 states | 143 city, municipal, and district councils |
| Mexico | 31 states, F.D. | 2,412 *municipios* |
| Mozambique | 10 provinces | 33 municipalities |
| Nepal | 75 districts and town panchayats | 4,022 village *panchayats* |
| Pakistan | 4 provinces | 15 municipal corporations, 457 municipal and town committees, 40 cantonment boards, 4,683 Union and district councils |
| Philippines | 76 *provinces* | 64 cities, 1,541 municipalities, 41,924 *barangays* |

*contd...*

*...contd...*

| Country | Intermediate | Local |
|---|---|---|
| Poland | 16 provinces, 307 poviats | 2,489 *gminas* |
| Russian Federation | 21 republics, 17 territories or autonomous areas, 49 provinces (oblasts), 2 cities of federal status | 1,868 *raions*, 650 first-tier cities, 26,766 secondary cities, townships, and villages |
| South Africa | 9 provinces | 850 local authorities |
| Thailand | 75 changwats, Bangkok | 6,397 districts, 148 municipalities and cities |
| Turkey | 74 provinces | 2,074 municipalities |
| Uganda | 45 districts, 13 municipalities | 950 sub counties, 39 municipal divisions, 51 town councils |
| Ukraine | 24 regions (oblasts), 1 autonomous republic, 2 municipalities | 619 districts |
| Venezuela | 23 states, F.D. | 282 municipalities |

*Note:* F.D. Federal district.

*Source:* World Development Report, 1999/2000.

# About PRIA

PRIA (Society for Participatory Research in Asia) is an International Centre for Learning and Promotion of Participation and Democratic Governance. Since its inception in 1982, PRIA has embarked on a set of key initiatives focusing on participatory research, citizen-centric development, capacity building, knowledge building and policy advocacy. With a combination of training, research and consultancy, it has grounded its work with conceptual rigour and understanding of social reality to command the strategic direction of interventions. PRIA works with a diverse range of partners at local, national and global levels.

PRIA's professional expertise and practical insights in the following areas are being utilised by other civil society groups, NGOs, governments, donors, trade unions, private business and academic institutions around the world:

- Participatory development methodologies,
- Institutional and human capacity building for social sector,
- Women's leadership and political empowerment,
- Empowerment of SC/ST leaders in *panchayats*,
- Citizen monitoring and social accountability of services,
- Participatory governance in *panchayats* and municipalities,
- Municipal reforms and participatory planning,
- Environmental and occupational health,
- Corporate social responsibility (CSR),
- Adult education and lifelong learning, and
- Gender mainstreaming in institutions (including preventing sexual harassment at workplace).

PRIA adopts three broad approaches in its ongoing programmes.

First, it intervenes directly in the field primarily in the northern and eastern poorer regions of India, in order to promote 'citizen's collective voices' to make demands on government institutions to claim their rights, access services and ensure accountable utilisation of public resources in development programmes. In recent years, PRIA's interventions have specially targeted Right to Information (RTI), National Rural Employment Guarantee Schemes (NREGS) and Urban Basic Services for Poor (UBSP).

Second, PRIA provides on-demand advisory and consultancy services to a wide variety of clients internationally. It utilises its practical knowledge and professional expertise in various areas to offer 'participatory and sustainable solutions' to improve supply sides of development and democracy.

Third, PRIA offers educational programmes in numerous human and social development themes, drawing from its field experiences, advisory services and extensive research projects. Within the framework of 'learning for social change', these educational courses are offered in distance modes, sometimes specially designed for a client and many times in partnership with such premier educational institutions as Indira Gandhi National Open University (IGNOU), India, University of Victoria (UVIC), Canada and Institute of Development Studies (IDS), UK.

Through its campaigns, research, education and policy advocacy interventions, PRIA's overarching mission is to 'make democracy work for all citizens'.